671
1

# Turkish Coffee
# and
# the Fertile Crescent

### Wanderings through the Lebanon, Mesopotamia, Israel, Jordan and Syria

*Also by Colette Modiano*
TWENTY SNOBS AND MAO

COLETTE MODIANO

# Turkish Coffee
# and
# the Fertile Crescent

## Wanderings through the Lebanon, Mesopotamia, Israel, Jordan and Syria

MICHAEL JOSEPH · London

First published in Great Britain by Michael Joseph Ltd.,
52 Bedford Square, London, WC1B 3EF
1974

© Colette Modiano 1974

ISBN 0 7181 1121 4

Set and printed in Great Britain by
Tonbridge Printers Ltd, Peach Hall Works, Tonbridge, Kent
in Garamond eleven on thirteen point,
and bound by James Burn at Esher, Surrey

# Contents

# Illustrations

To NICHOLAS

# Introduction

SINCE my first visit in 1967 I have returned many times to Palestine and made several journeys into Mesopotamia. I have jumped at any excuse, an invitation from an Arab or Israeli friend. Seeking whatever truth is hidden among the tangled passions and hatreds, prejudices and traditions, I have stifled my opinions and set aside preconceptions. The rewards are always worth while, often great. I believe that I have been unbiased. I used not to feel emotionally involved in the conflict. I do now, for I feel for both sides – which is hardly comfortable, but I am in good company. Diplomats, writers, journalists, tourists if lucky, have left their hearts on Palestine's fragile human frontiers. 'Our lives will never be the same again,' the French ambassador to Israel told me with undisguised emotion.

# *Jordan*

THE road was uneven, and the rolling landscape seemed made of dust. It was eight o'clock on a warm February morning in Amman. The city now had seventy thousand refugees to look after, as well as the quarter of a million people who normally lived there in the capital of a kingdom which since the Six-Day War had only the infertile half of her 34,750 square miles but still had to feed nine-tenths of her previous population of 2,200,000.

The aerodrome was noisy and squalid, the staff fierce, with aggressive moustaches and their heads covered with large red-and-white-check *keffiehs*, held in place with black silk laces. The police wore black uniforms and unexpected pike helmets like souvenirs of the First World War. In fact, they were a hangover from the Turkoman invasion in the thirteenth century and had acquired rear-peaks against the climate. The gigantic sentry, with sandy hair, a ruddy complexion, and eyes as blue as the sky, was a Devonshire man if ever I saw one, yet when I spoke to him in English he replied in Arabic. West countrymen must have been through these parts. I climbed gingerly into my taxi with a begrimed and dishevelled and rather repulsive driver. It was an austere and poverty-stricken scene: bare hills covered with little stone houses, yet with a grave beauty from the ochre earth baking in the harsh light. The streets of Amman were made of mud and there was a good deal of noisy traffic in the main thoroughfare, ancient American cars covered with dust, motor bikes, and one old man bent double under a cageful of hens. Old two- or three-storey houses lined the narrow pavements. The crowd was thick but all men, there was not a woman to be seen. Here and there were Jordanian soldiers in their British uniforms and though the shops' names were in Arabic there was the odd English word like 'Hairdresser' and 'Bank of Jordan'. We passed bookshops, cloth merchants, tiny engineering work-shops, and innumerable barbers, each with its candy-striped pole. In the Middle East, a man visits the barber every day. Through a haze of noise, dust and sunlight, the taxi ground up a hill where the street suddenly broadened into a spacious avenue with large houses, and the traffic flowed more easily. This was the residential quarter of stone mansions topped with colourful roof-gardens, and well-guarded official buildings. The Jordan Hotel is the local Intercontinental with 'all mod. cons' in the best American tradition. I ordered a bottle of Evian water at seventy pence and tucked into my third breakfast. Sirens began to wail as if they would never stop, and I counted ten or more explosions. Well, I had been warned by the Embassy that the situation was 'less than ideal for the would-be tourist'.

Ariane had arrived earlier and the doorman found us a well-upholstered American car which we sank into without wasting a moment. Our driver was tall, swarthy and engaging. His name was Moses, but he wasn't a Jew. He was from Nablus in Cisjordan, and he exploded at the mention of King Hussein: 'A foreigner, a British hireling. Even married an Englishwoman . . . Betraying his country . . . The British are supporting Israel . . .'

The victim of this contemptuous abuse was the only Arab leader to offer a home to his compatriots, the Palestinian refugees pouring out of Cisjordan over twenty-five years. In 1948 there were already nearly 700,000 of them. Today there are roughly a million and a half, and the majority are implacable enemies of the Hashemites, despising their 'treacherously' accommodating attitude towards Israel. They forget that Syria and Iraq, though wealthy states, have given no succour to the refugees and often

14

imprison the luckless few who try to settle there. Lebanon has simply shut her eyes and ears to the problem, preferring to sit on the fence rather than to jeopardize the fragile balance of her mixed population.

Only Hussein, the 'murderer', the 'hireling', has absorbed the hapless people, and his reward has been full-scale revolution which he quelled by napalm and mortar shells. His ruthless restoration of law and order made him the scapegoat of the Baathist states, who claimed to be deeply moved by the plight of the unfortunate refugees. Oil-producing Kuwait and Saudi Arabia even cut off Jordan's supplies in the spring of 1970. It was a cruel measure and broke Jordan's economy. Windswept wastes – unlike oil – have little market value.

Hussein's brother-Arabs were unmoved: as far as they were concerned, the refugees could die and so could Hussein, just like his grandfather Abdullah, a man 'too intelligent' to play Telemachus at Lawrence's side. Abdullah's consolation prize, however, was awarded 'with a stroke of a pen, on a Sunday afternoon in Cairo', when Churchill created the emirate of Transjordan whose 150,000 Bedouin inhabitants were passionately devoted to the new emir.

Abdullah had regard for Golda Meir, the chief Jewish negotiator, and tried to come to terms with the Jews. Under the partition agreement of 1948 he acquired the eastern side of Palestine and his enlarged emirate became a kingdom. On 10 July 1951, outside the El Aqsa mosque in Jerusalem, he appointed his fifteen-year-old grandson as his successor. A few days later Abdullah was assassinated by a Moslem Brother as he emerged from the same mosque.

We left Amman and drove across a vast, brown, rocky plain, towards an immense white shell, the King Hussein stadium, large enough to train the entire Arab Legion for the five thousand metres. Some people argue that the money would have been better spent on irrigation or on housing the Palestinian refugees whose camp lies only a few miles away, where 180,000 of them live on a high plateau with no sturdier shelter than crude shanties improvised from straw, cardboard, corrugated iron, oil-drums and bits of blanket. Some scratching dogs, scraggy chickens, and hopeful goats snuffled among the broken stones. The children waved and laughed as the car went by, like children everywhere, but the women, shrouded in black, only stared at us. During 1969, the camp swelled week by week as the terror-stricken families fled from the Israeli attacks on the frontier zone. The summers are torrid, the winters icy, and the waves of repression ruthless but there is one problem these people do not face: the problem of space. The desert is limitless. They would starve but for funds from U.N.W.R.A. By now there is a generation deprived of their hereditary farming skills but without any other trade. At school, their heads are filled with biased propaganda by teachers who are themselves refugees. Again and again they are urged towards the Djihad, the Holy War, and these exhortations, wordy and incoherent, are sustained with snippets from Mao's Little Red Book. Propaganda on this scale, working with poverty, idleness and despair, implants a desperate hunger for revolutionary action. It was in Wahadat and other camps surrounding Amman that the Palestinian refugees became a guerrilla force. Here, harassed by the sun and wind, they trained; here they mounted guard with implacable will, and their tents became a solid bulwark which the king's loyal Bedouins were unable to breach. Yet the revolt found no leader, no human focal point, and it has collapsed in spite of its often heroic, sometimes grotesque efforts. Choukeiry's spluttering and mindless rantings made him 'Israel's best ally', and his reptilian successor, Arafat, had three chins instead of a political head. Despite this absence of a leader, there was a time when Middle East experts thought little of Hussein's chances and expected the guerrillas to win a war in which they had, after all, nothing to lose.

Emerging from these desperate wastes, the road winds through mimosa and eucalyptus downhill to Jerash – the Gerasa of Alexander the Great – where the huge oval forum is ringed with

Roman colonnades and paved with its original flagstones. An avenue of ruined pillars hugs the hillside, among thorn-bushes and wild narcissus.

In Gerasa's turbulent history it was conquered by Jews and by Pompey. In the fourth century, it was a Christian diocese before the Byzantine emperor Justinian covered it with churches. It was destroyed in the seventh century by the Sassanian Persians and then by the Arabs. In the thirteenth century, earthquakes and the efforts of the Frankish king Baldwin II, razed the city to the ground. Six centuries later, it became a haven for Circassian refugees from southern Russia, who used the ancient stones to build their new houses. Their descendants today are an exclusive caste of wealthy landowners, holding high office. They form the king's personal bodyguard and their glittering uniforms recall Czarist Russia. How alien such finery was to the feddayeen fighting pitched battles in September 1970 against Hussein's Bedouins, when Artemis's temple became a barricade and Jerash an armed stronghold!

Only a few olive-trees cast mean shadows over the felled and broken columns lying among the weeds. It was soothingly peaceful. We were the only visitors except for a policeman following us step by step, particularly interested in me and my obsession with archaeology. I was kneeling beside every stone, poring over every relief, and scraping every promising bit of débris with the rusted blade of an old pen-knife. Antics like these confuse the Jordanian police. This particular officer was a solid, striking-looking, well-scrubbed man in his fifties, sweating slightly in his dark blue uniform. He seemed weary: sad, even. It would have been much easier for him to come along with us instead of lurking in our wake. I invited him, insisting that we had no intention of stealing treasures or laying mines. We were French, I told him. There was an ecstatic 'Ah! General de Gaulle!'

As we approached the ruins of Artemis's temple our new friend told us that he was Palestinian and had lived in Jerusalem until the siege of 1948. What a melancholy and ironic fate: a man stripped of his roots, living in an anguished and truncated kingdom, spending his days guarding the ephemeral relics of a distant past!

His English was slow and he groped for words. 'Yes,' he said, 'I am now quite used to living in Transjordan. I live in Amman, I have three children. I earn a good wage. Yes, I like King Hussein. No, the king's decisions are not influenced by the British. No, the guerrillas will not make it easier to establish peace with Israel. Oh yes, I miss Jerusalem.' His voice broke. 'Yes, I would like to go back, but only if we can live there as we did in the past. I would not like to go there as a visitor . . . Sometimes a man must make a new start . . .'

He fell behind us again as Ariane and I climbed the slope to the ruins of the ancient theatre which dominated the Circassian village strung out along the facing hillside. The Circassians, the Cherkas . . . Here were the dreams of childhood – brave handsome heroes astride their horses, silver-frogged and charging the flames.


There is a gentle joy and strange harmony in the graceful curve of the forum, the long majestic avenue stretching through the valley, the white village touched by the golden light of the late afternoon and, over all, the pungent smell of wild plants. Coming out of my dream, I saw that our policeman still had a sharp but friendly eye on us from below. We returned with him to the car, and joined him for a drink at the small café.


'What crime these Jews have committed. Instead of being generous, they adopted policies of systematic terrorism and repression.'

These sentiments came from a handsome man with oyster-coloured eyes cast in grief towards the ceiling. The French ambassador was as gloomy as his beautiful white stone house.

His views were tartly supported by a short, bald-headed figure introduced to me as the Amman correspondent of French Television. 'It's the Israelis' fault, right enough. In 1969 they bombed all the frontier villages, one bomb for each village, to intimidate the population thoroughly. Don't forget they used napalm.' He wheezed into his next argument. 'Over seventy thousand refugees came to Amman, all of them hostile to the king, who promptly penned them up in camps like the notorious Wahadat, which his Bedouins then pounded during the Civil War of 1970.'

He riled me, this little man with a face full of venom. Even if his words were true, his tone was tendentious. The affected voice of a minor member of the ambassador's staff interjected, 'A pity they pressed for direct negotiations in 1967.'

Then the television man burned with indignation again. 'Sinking the fishing-boats of the Gaza Arabs only robbed innocent refugees of their livelihood.'

Surely he knew that the Gaza fishing fleet had run guns and terrorists from Egypt for the Palestine Liberation Army? No one mentioned this. You would have thought the vessels carried innocent sardines. 'The Jews did things even the Germans shrank from. When they arrested someone, they blew up the building.'

The discussion grew louder. How passionately this war re-echoes in people's minds! One understands the Arabs and the Jews, but that this intensity should exist among Americans, British, French, Russians! I can tell by the way they say 'Jew', 'Arab', 'Jerusalem', what these words mean deep inside them. Often, I hear only the veiled sound of 'wog' and 'yid'. The prejudices are there before the cards are on the table. Whenever racism appears in drawing-room urbanities, neat arguments melt away like frost under a hot sun, and from there on it is hard to hold the truth. It would take a Buddha not to groan under exaggeration and insult. I was after all in the East.

Moses collected us, punctual as always and we roller-coastered up and down the hills. The little white square houses, some of stone but mostly of white-washed bricks, gave the landscape rhythm and harmony. The smell of the East is a sun-baked medley of dust, spice, orange, olive and coffee. The royal palace is concealed by trees, and the avenue leading to it was blocked by a Jordanian army post where the soldiers aimed their sub-machine-guns at our midriffs. No chance of getting past men like these! The museum was closed as it was Friday, the day of the Prophet. On a hilltop above the town, however, stands a huge Roman theatre, a relic of the ancient city of Philadelphia. Another navy-blue policeman shouted at some grinning locals who were gathering round to beg, and he soon sent them away.

Moses invited us to his house for coffee. Ariane was reluctant. She did not want to put him to so much trouble. But his wife was expecting us and I told Ariane that he was just being nice and it would be interesting. I pushed her towards the car.

We drove through a maze of unpaved streets and shabby houses. Most had tiled roofs, though some were only crudely protected with corrugated iron. The odd stunted tree shaded a doorway, and here and there we saw prickly pears. The gardens were strewn with old tyres, tin cans and rubbish. Shrill children were playing with toy carts made from a few bits of wood knocked together. Two of them stopped and stared at us with big brown eyes. They were Moses's son and daughter and this poor, clean little house was his home. An open cistern toilet was on the right of the front door, and, on the left, was the kitchen where I glimpsed a miniature stove with two aluminium saucepans and a few bowls. The main room beyond was lit by a bare, overhead bulb. There were carpets and several beds with cheerful cotton counterpanes. Moses' wife brought us coffee. Her chubby, bright-eyed face was enchanting but she was very much overweight, with a drooping bosom. She wore a large white scarf and a long floral skirt with a black apron. She was twenty-five and Moses forty-two. Their marriage had been arranged by their families. She regarded him with an air of submissive adoration. Moses, fond and protective, patted her thigh. Meanwhile, Ariane whooped and gurgled with a robust baby nestling under a bedspread, and this lent substance to our halting conversation. Moses

20

was well-satisfied with his life in Amman. He had security and the work was lively and varied. His wife was from a village on the West Bank. He said he would never go back to Nablus, not to live anyway, though he might pay a visit. All things considered, they were a happy couple, sitting side by side, with their open faces and ready smiles.

Architectural order ended abruptly at the city boundary but the women were still clad like their sisters in Amman – old women in black veils and girls in translucent white muslin with the occasional glimpse of a large eye rimmed with kohl.

The intense light burnt my western eyes in that flat, flinty, endless desert. The road wound up the mountains, past Madaba, where Moses insisted that we should see a mosaic floor from the time of Justinian. It had an enchanting design of rivers, dromedaries, sheep and palm-trees.

We picnicked on a high cliff looking down on the rocks of Wadi Mudjib. Our crumbs flew off into the boundless, fractured landscape. Below us, were the thin thread of the Jordan, the Dead Sea, a small blue lake, and beyond, Jericho, a purple shadow! Strange country of legendary names where from the bare soil came man's greatest inspiration and from desert tents grew a spiritual life loftier than any known before. I imagined the herds, the Moabite tribes and the Nabataeans who battled with them; waves of Roman legions; Crusaders with the motley throng that travelled in their wake. The land hums with the life, battles, aspirations and creeds of its past.

An army detachment took away our passports before we reached the outskirts of Kerak where the ruins of the mightiest fortresses in Christendom still stand on a sharp-edged plateau surrounded by ravines. Ariane and I like tiny specks, looked down on the pink and ochre mountains of the surrounding desert. We could see the stony bed of the meandering Wedi Mousa which provides the only water in the region. I rested my hand on those walls which had once rung with the roars of the Castellan, Reynold of

Chatillon. Handsome, hot-blooded and cruel, despised by his peers, devoid of scruples or political ability, rashly and bloodily he brought about the downfall of the Frankish kingdom, whose policy had been to play on the Moslems' dissensions, encouraging them to regard the kingdom of Jerusalem as a stabilizing influence and the king as a useful arbiter.

Reynold was an adventurer who came to the Holy Land in 1153, in the wake of Louis VII. A younger son, without land or fortune, he seduced and married Constance, the young widow of Raymond of Poitiers. Through one political blunder after another, he warred with the Armenians, whose alliance – like that of Byzantium – was essential to the balance of power and to peace. He sacked the Byzantine island of Cyprus, looting, raping, cutting-off ears and noses, and earning the implacable hatred of Christians and Moslems. He was finally taken prisoner in 1160 by Nureddin and for sixteen years he rotted in jail at Aleppo. Within months of his release, he married Etiennette, widow of the king's councillor, Miles of Plancy. She was the junoesque mistress of the wealthiest landowner in the region. They said she looked 'like the biggest tower' in her castle of Kerak, whose fortifications were Reynold's obsession.

Ruthless brigands from every corner of the kingdom banded together under his command and no questions were asked. In 1181, Reynold plunged into the Negeb, attacking a caravan of dromedaries laden with gold, silver, tapestries and provisions, thus incurring the wrath of both Baldwin IV and Saladin – no mean combination. Saladin promptly threw his mamelukes against Kerak. It was on the point of falling to Saladin when the Frankish army appeared, led by King Baldwin, who was in the final stages of leprosy and too weak to rise from his litter. Seeing his stricken and honourable foe, Saladin retired so that the king might die undefeated.

As we approached Petra, Ariane had eaten enough to satisfy a small army and the car smelled of rancid butter, turning my stomach on the twists and turns of the desert road. I managed a sound which might have been taken for a laugh.

'What's funny?' she asked 'Are you hungry?'

'I suppose you realize you've two hours' hard riding ahead of you?'

'Oh, no!' she cried. 'I can't stand horses. They petrify me.'

My snide retort took the edge off my temper. When we reached the rest-house I even suggested a stop for coffee. The steeds were surprisingly tractable and Ariane recovered her equanimity. We set off along a narrow defile, hemmed in by jagged rocks with the sky like a thin blue ribbon above us. We passed a tomb and two Doric columns carved in the rocks and then the track grew narrower so that we had to ride single file. Other tombs in a high wall of red rock looked like temples with their columns and pilasters and friezes. Fantastic and oppressive, they weighed down above our shivering little troop. A few years earlier, twenty tourists had been swept away by a sudden inexplicable torrent.

A lone Swiss traveller named Burckhardt found these Nabataean remains in 1912. The Nabataeans were strange people, merchants and caravaneers who came from Saudi Arabia, speaking Aramaic, like Christ; their city, Petra, was so famed that the conquering Pompey made it an imperial residence. It declined from the third century when caravans were lured away to pass by Palmyra.

On horses like ours, Burckhardt had picked his way through these rocks, when suddenly the road gave out and he found himself before a temple protruding from an enormous red cliff and standing golden in the sunlight. We saw it yard by yard at each bend in the pass until it stood glowing like a giant ruby in its vast, dreamlike plateau, a plateau exploding with tall red rocks veined with brown, white and blue, so that the façades of the temple looked like stupendous spheres of agate. A short, steep rise leads to the colonnaded front of the law-court, where the huge interior has been scooped out of the rock and you can see on the walls the notches that once held rings for the prisoners' chains. We passed alone from one valley to another, lunar travellers in a desert desolation. There were Nabataean cave-

homes where the inmates had huddled at night, warming themselves at large fires burning in the middle of the floor where the
smoke judging by the blackness of the ceilings escaped erratically
through the doorway. As we came down from our lunar heights,
we passed the only other human being in these infinite spaces: a
colourful peasant girl, fine-featured and unveiled, who was
squatting, with her baby beside her, displaying Nabataean terracotta cups, vases and larmiers. Some had been found at the foot of
the hills after landslides caused by rain and others in the bed of
streams. I bought a number and carried them in my canvas hat.

Ariane was by now quite sprightly on her old nag and the
ride back seemed to end all too soon. Petra was a place apart, a
strange, dramatic, petrified world that left me silent and disturbed.

It was already night, and a little wearily I watched the moon on
the rocks overhanging the road. Lawrence, with his Bedouins, his
dromedaries and his friend Dahoum, must have camped close by.
It was here, wrapped in his *keffieh* that he found escape, cause
and purpose.

A brilliant mass of lights appeared on our right. It was not
Aqaba, but Eilat. The road wound between craggy rocks until we
could see the smaller lights of Aqaba. The port was closed. Everyone had moved away since the war.

We made short work of a well-served meal in an overlit
dining-room among a handful American and English tourists on a
week-end trip from Amman. The starry night, the lapping waves,
the scent of the flowers, the lights of nearby Eilat – within
seconds I was blissfully asleep.

The golden sand trickled through my fingers and the white sun
burned my eyes. Moses had vanished to make his report.

The dust came from the Syrian phosphates on the jetties
stacked and waiting to be loaded on cargo-boats from Aqaba –
which, unbelievably, was Jordan's only point of contact with the
outside world, apart from the Allenby Bridge. This absurd situation had existed since Syria and Iraq had broken off relations.

24

Aqaba's lively, narrow streets were full of stalls of dress materials, tinned food, fruit, patties, spices, almond cakes and *halva,* that exquisite mixture of honey and almonds. We munched greedily, chattering with delight. Ariane bought a dressing-gown from China, worthy of Sulka and costing no more than seventy-five pence. I found an enchanting blue glazed kettle from Poland and I carried it like a handbag till I got back to Paris.

I was still obsessed by the image of Lawrence riding like the wind at the head of his Bedouins, and we wanted to spend a few hours following in his footsteps.

The Aqaba Beach Hotel offered us a car for ten Jordanian pounds as ours was in danger of falling apart. The Rest House offered us one for eight. A taxi-driver said we could have one for seven, and showed us a filthy blue vehicle which, he said, was his brother's. We accepted it without much enthusiasm.

Back at the hotel, Moses was lolling in a deck-chair and he claimed he had been waiting for us all day. He tried to redeem himself by offering a car for five pounds. In the event, there was only one car to which each contractor had added his own profit.

We left Aqaba in our five-pound Land-Rover. A police officer stopped us and grabbed our passports. When Moses spoke up, I caught the word 'Frankaoui,' which the officer repeated; his manner softened abruptly. He smiled, bowed, returned our passports and climbed proprietorily into the Land-Rover, followed by a soldier armed to the teeth with revolvers and sub-machine-guns. After a third of a mile, he stopped us again. Some Bedouin tents were too close to an army encampment. He bawled and waved his arms. We left the road for a track which cut across a stony plain. The rocky mountains formed strange outlines in the indigo sky. Gold and mauve, some were shaped like citadels and others like great beasts; charred patches marked old craters and Bedouins crouched by their camels, dozing in the heat. It was through this jagged, tawny, never-ending pass that Lawrence swept on 2 July 1918, 'riding like a madman and discharging his pistol at the Turks'. The purpose of the operation was to attack the enemy in the rear, dislodge them from the hills, seize the arms they had just unloaded, and carry them off for the conquest of Damascus. On 5 July his Bedouins stormed the heights of Aqaba, slaughtering the Turkish troops; the following day, they took the town itself. Lawrence, anxious as always for his extraordinary legend, darted across a hundred and fifty miles of desert to Cairo to announce his triumph in person.

Near the Saudi Arabian border were half a dozen armed cameleers drinking coffee at the foot of a small, crenellated fort of paddled clay. They were not forgotten extras from Lawrence of Arabia, but desert police, handsome, very dark, imposing men with the    traditional red-and-white Jordanian *keffieh,* supple leather riding boots, and long, skirted garments gathered at the waist by cartridge belts. Each belt had its dagger and a full complement of bullets. They spread carpets on the sand and invited us to sit, presenting us with small mugs of coffee from a copper urn. It was so bitter that I came perilously close to pulling a face. Ariane grinned at me. When our mugs were empty, our hosts recharged them again and again – and always with the most engaging smiles. Finally Moses rescued us, explaining that the custom is to sway the mug from side to side several times. I did so with a sigh of relief, as I had begun to feel queasy and Ariane's cheeks were turning green. Two of these charming companions appeared to have designs on us. I whispered to Ariane, who is at least five months my senior, 'Why, you're old enough to be their mother!' 'You're just jealous of my figure,' she replied. Our new flames hoisted us on to camels; which restored my zest for life. The combination of desert and dromedary has a magical, exhilarating effect on me. I could almost see myself as a Lawrence. Afterwards we were shown over the little fort, bristling with rifles and machine-guns, but not allowed to photograph it. From a makeshift billet with three unmade beds, at the top of a narrow staircase, we looked over a superb view. And then, with endless smiles, thanks, snapshots and *salam alekums,* we took our leave.

Two men in grey suits trudged towards the fort. Their presence was odd, to say the least. Moses, his rear pocket bulging with the fattest revolver I have ever seen, abandoned us without a word, loping off towards them. The trio conversed, Moses with an air of authority, while the others listened and nodded. Moses had a pretty assertive manner for an ordinary Jordanian chauffeur. His dealings with the police and military were always marked with this quality. No doubt we were being watched, but it did not trouble me, so long as we could be sure of official protection.

'Friends of yours?' I asked Moses.

'No, no.'

'Guerrillas, then?' I said, smiling so innocently that I must have looked mentally deficient.

'I don't think so.'

He looked surprised, as if the possibility had never occurred to him.

We returned to Amman on the new highway, a road running so straight that Hussein's enemies claimed that he built it specially for his Maserati. Every six miles or so, soldiers ordered us to show our passports. Our French nationality served us well: it always did, in Arab countries. A few months later, in northern Egypt, I was to be greeted with the cry of 'Bibidigol'* Today it was simply "Digol, Digol!'

Past King Hussein Stadium again, where, in 1970, during the Civil War, a short, witty diplomat called Mérillon, set up the French field-hospital and saved hundreds of Palestinian lives. He held the king in high esteem. 'I like the job,' Hussein had told him one day. 'Sire,' said Mérillon, 'the French hospital is said to be the guerrillas' hospital, it is true. But since it *is* a French hospital, would Your Majesty honour it with a visit?' The king agreed, none too happily. Mérillon drove to the Stadium and spelt out his orders to the guerrillas. 'You will applaud him not loudly, not for long. But you will applaud him. And no one, repeat no one, is to take a shot at him!' The time for the visit arrived. The king shook a few hands, without

* 'Vive de Gaulle!'

smiling. The guerrillas applauded. Not loudly, not for long.
But they applauded.

A last walk through the teeming city, so austere and so hospitable. I lingered by an old bookshop, with shelves of Arabic
literature and English translations of Maupassant. I peered into
a barber's where the customers, swathed in robes and turbans
looked like snowmen as the dexterously wielded blade swooped
over their proffered throats, making a silken murmur as it glided
over the skin. Old men in *arabayas* and young ones in trousers
and white shirt all flowed past me, unruffled and strangely
silent, staring hard at me, not, alas! at my beauty but because
I happened to be the only woman in the street so late and was,
moreover, wearing trousers. I felt embarrassed, but they were
inquisitive more than derisive, and without hostility. Xenophobia
comes and goes in the Middle East, but I have always, in Jordan
or elsewhere, met with niceness, friendliness and warmth.

Moses gave us a hearty send-off at the airport. He shook our
hands for a long time, and I felt melancholic too as he walked
sturdily away, his huge revolver jutting from his back-pocket.
Soon we were flying over the seven hills and the rugged landscape, sanctified by the indelible mark of its people and their
conflicts, hopes and faiths.

# *Iraq*

IN the sticky heat of a pair of low-roofed buildings, dark except for some meagre lights, six members of the immigration tribunal, present masters of our fate, were seated at a raised desk. Four were soldiers: one of the others, shabby and tie-less, was hectoring me into buying Iraqi Red Cross stamps. They were all rather daunting figures, with their dark skins and warlike moustaches. They glowered in turn at my passport as it passed from hand to hand. At last, it came back to me. Ariane's, how-ever, was promptly confiscated. She had obtained her visa in Cyprus, the main traffic-junction between Israel and the Arab states.

Iraqi and Syrian officials are intensely mistrustful of papers rubber-stamped in Cyprus and regard them almost as suspiciously as they do Israeli visas. Fortunately a representative of the French embassy was waiting for us in the baggage-hall, for I had begun to feel on edge. Customs men, the same colour as the khaki walls, went through our belongings, taking the back off Ariane's camera and running their dirty hands all over my light-coloured dresses. The sight of the *Guide Bleu* disturbed them and they alerted their boss, who stared at it and then darkly at me. Mr Moussa, our guardian-angel from the embassy, looked tense, but Ariane retrieved her passport.

The evening air clung to our faces like a hot, wet handker-chief. Down a poorly-lit avenue which a Turkish general had blasted in 1915 so that he could deploy his artillery against the

29

British, we arrived at the Baghdad Palace. The entrance hall was stately and the receptionist efficient, but there were some shady figures lurking by the door. Moussa whispered, 'You will have to be careful. The place is full of spies and microphones.' I, in turn, whispered his warning to Ariane.

I woke next morning in the warmth of a pale sunlight which raised an opalescent haze from the muddy waters of the Tigris. With the English breakfast came the *Baghdad Observer* announcing four C.I.A. spies to be executed today . . . Eight Israelies killed in gun battle with Jordanians – no Jordanian casualties. And on an inside page, 'Veterinarians' conference pledges full support for Palestine Liberation Front'. The guerrillas' livestock might have felt friskier at this news had the guerrillas owned any livestock. There was a well-presented survey of the Italian fashion scene and an impenetrable piece on economics. I rang Ariane for her reactions and saw a bugging device on the back of the telephone. Feeling a little like James Bond, I searched the room: there was a second microphone nestling in the bedside lamp. Ariane's voice came on the line. 'What a lovely view!' I said blandly. 'What a really good hotel, and aren't the people nice?'

Later, with Moussa, we wandered through the deserted museum, with its statues, bas-reliefs, pottery, jewellery, furniture from Ur and Khorsabad, Nineveh and Babylon. Sumptuous, delicate and evocative, here was a highly developed civilization dating back to the fourth millennium B.C. Six thousand years ago this parched, barren waste had been an Eden, with a vigorous, refined, artistic and intellectual life. We lingered at the face of an Akkad king, a Sumerian harp from Ur surmounted by a ram's head wrought in gold, a presentation scene in the court of Sargon II, where the figures almost sprang from the wall. Paul Emile Botta must have seen them like that on the walls of Sargon's palace at Dur-Sharrukin, now known as Khorsabad, in Northern Iraq. As French consul in the 1840s he initiated all the great digs within the river valleys of the Tigris and the Euphrates. His successor, Victor Place, who shared the dig at Nineveh with Henry Creswicke Rawlinson, entrusted two hundred and thirty-five packing cases of their finds to four *keleks,* simple wooden rafts buoyed up by air-filled goatskin bottles. Alas, Arab insurgents attacked the convoy at Qurna, where the Tigris and the Euphrates meet, and the *keleks* went to the bottom with their priceless load, so that today one of the great bulls of Khorsabad is buried in the mud of the Tigris.

Dazed, I was picking my way from case to case among the gold jewels which Sir Leonard Woolley brought from the royal cemetery at Ur in 1922, when four soldiers burst into the silence and vanished as suddenly as they had appeared. In the hot, dirty street, Ariane confessed that she still had a pocketful of Israeli coins. I thrust them into my handbag, intending to get rid of them as soon as possible. From another pocket, she offered me a tube of Pepsodent toothpaste, with the brand-name printed in Hebrew characters so huge that I felt sure everyone in the city could see them. Ariane was attempting, so far without success, to track down two veterans of the '48 War. The war was inescapable here, and all conversations seemed to come back to it. Here, as in any other police state, people talked about the past more readily than the present.

We drove all over Mansur, the Neuilly of Baghdad, with its large avenues of roses and bougainvillea, searching for the house of Jabra Ibrahim Jabra. At last we found it, and were shown into a large room, with long grey couches, wide low tables, tall lamps, and walls covered with book-shelves and paintings. It was restful and welcoming. Jabra Ibrahim Jabra joined us at once, tall and elegant. His hair was long and his accent was English. We talked, avoiding the minefield of Iraqi politics, and our host picked his words with care, but it was clear from the start that he was not bigoted and was open-minded. His early years had been spent in Palestine but, after teaching at Harvard, he had come to Baghdad, where he was a professor at the university and used his influence to promote interest in modern art and literature. He wrote poems and novels in Arabic, and one novel has been published in English. The paintings around us were the work of young Iraqi artists.

His wife joined us, a cheerful, high-spirited Iraqi, with a long flowing garment over her full figure. She eagerly dashed to the telephone a dozen times to help Ariane find her two war-heroes. We sipped cool drinks, talking but not about the problem of Iraq or the Middle East. We might equally well have been in California or Provence.

Mme Jabra soon solved Ariane's problem with times and places for meeting the two men. One of them, it seemed, was a retired general and the father of a friend. The other had become a drunk and a tramp.

We drove back through the poorer district, where the crowds were thicker, with women shrouded in black veils, and men in black and white *keffiehs* with loose jackets over the *arabayas* flapping like nightshirts. They stood about in groups near the bitter music from the cafés. Road-surfacing was a battered memory, street-planning a vague hope. Workmen bellowed at one another, examining a gaping hole, a sewage-system suffering from one of those unaccountable fits of temperament that afflict sewage-systems. Filthy and muddy, the city lolls beside the Tigris, ironwork rusting on the balconies, paint peeling from the walls.

In the evening, there was a recital by an Iraqi woman pianist of Armenian extraction. I watched the audience arrive, mostly the bourgeoisie, some enlightened, some wealthy, some perhaps both. The women were short and plump in black or white, glittering with a restraint appropriate to the Baathist régime. Their men were perfect complements, in white shirts, dark suits and sober ties. There was a sprinkling of foreigners, a group of monks two by two, some nuns. A wave of bowing and scraping preceded the Armenian patriarch, with his white beard and purple head-dress. The Armenian colony, chiefly town-people, is a thriving, active force in Iraq.

Western ambassadors conversed in the well-upholstered front seats. Their wives are seldom to be seen east of Beirut: they remain in Europe, oddly prone to mysterious illnesses. The hefty charmer launched into Couperin, captivating the exotic audience with the precise and precious echoes of the French king's court, whose flights of wit had matched the sprightly tones of the small, frail keyboards. This music, so very French, so curiously out of place in such surroundings, reminded us how far away we were, among the marked-places of the East, almost as far as India: around us was Asia, warm-toned, remote, smiling, enigmatic.

We came out into a icy wind which was stabbing and buffeting the sand, so that we could scarcely see the headlights and streetlamps. The director of the French Cultural Centre mentioned a Feydeau play they were rehearsing. Feydeau and Couperin in Baghdad! The director talked of his French-language students with real affection. He had once asked a young Iraqi why he studied French. The student said, 'For telephone purposes.' 'A career in the Post Office?' the director wondered. 'No,' the student answered, it was to help tap calls. Apparently he thought the job would be better done if he knew more words and phrases; he was often detailed to tap the director's telephone.

The wind kept up, and by morning the city was yellow with sand, as was the embassy. Over coffee, the ambassador gave me a survey of Iraq. Bright-eyed and precise, he explained her isolation, the result of her geographical position and her poor road, rail and air communications. Her trade was by caravans on the desert between Mesopotamia and India, or by cargo ships from Basra, on the Shatt al Arab river, a few miles from the Persian border. The Indian line (la Malle des Indes) once called at Basra, but not now. Sealed off from attitudes of the modern world, Iraq retains her medieval mentality: hence the hangings which Europeans cannot understand. The ambassador insisted that revolutions in Iraq are not especially bloody. It was true that King Faisal and eight members of his family were killed in the uprising of 14 July 1958, but the general tendency was to imprison opponents rather than kill them! This policy has been pursued by successive governments. The ambassador is a very nice man, and I admired the warm affection with which he defended his hosts and their forbears, but I was not convinced. For centuries, purging has taken a grim form, and the long record of domestic strife contains some particularly horrifying dates. In 693, while fifty thousand men and thirty thousand women were jailed by the ruler, Ibn-Yussuf, a hundred and thirty thousand were put to death. In 883, the Zends, former slaves from Zanzibar, who shovelled the polluting nitrates of the Shatt al Arab, rebelled and were tortured, mutilated, flogged and publicly hanged. In 930, a Qarmat leader, Mansur Halladj, was lashed five hundred times: his feet were cut off, he was crucified and left hanging all night.

The inhabitants have a natural aptitude for atrocities which invaders have done little to soften. In 1931, Ismet Inony put down a major revolt by the Kurds, whose dreams of independence had been fostered by the British in World War I. Pierre Rossi, a journalist, described the results of Inonu's measures: 'Lines of gallows stood silhouetted against the canopy of hills, the ravines of Kiar Bekir echoed with the sound of firing squads. In 1933, the Iraqi army burned sixty villages; six hundred Assyrians were machine-gunned or bayoneted to death, and the remainder were deported.'

The British Consul, Monck Mason, was hacked to pieces six years later by an intemperate crowd in Mosul and four Communist leaders were hanged in 1947, three of them in public.

In the revolution of 14 July 1958, the Hashemite royal family lost nine of its members including the king and the crowd dangled what was left of the Prince Royal from a cornice of the Ministry of Defence.

In 1959, General Kassem reacted so vigorously to the revolt headed by General Chawaf that the writer Larry Collins tells me that he personally counted twenty-nine gallows in the city.

The government, headed by General El Bakr, hanged fourteen unnamed persons on 14 August 1970, casting a chill over the Conference of Arab States which was then meeting in Cairo.

Egypt's semi-official newspaper, *Al-Ahram* spoke of the 'unappetizing spectacle of the gallows erected in Revolution Square, Baghdad'.

M. de Favières, charming and erudite French Cultural Attaché, told me that human life did not have the same value for the Iraqis as it had for us, and that we should avoid judging them by our standards – the public spectacle of death was simply for intimidation, no other reason. The mob lived in greater terror than the government, which has ample historical reason for fearing revolt. As for those fourteen hangings which caused so much bother in the outside world, over half who died were non-Jewish: they were put to death inside the prison and only their remains were strung up in Tahrir Square.

Which, of course, makes all the difference.

There is little grace in the buildings stretching along the wide avenues. The paving-stones are large and uneven, like those I played hopscotch on as a child. The air of a little provincial city was reinforced by the motor traffic and the elderly ass-drivers urging on their sad, rough-coated beasts with long bamboo sticks.

In Tahrir Square, known as Liberation Square, I felt the unease I had felt at the airport. Iraq scared me a little, in a way I have never felt in other authoritarian states. One could so easily picture a gallows among the street-lamps or hear the roars and shrieks of a mob, even though the people looked harmless enough.

I persuaded Ariane that we would be far better off with a chauffeur-driven car, as the chauffeur would also serve as guide, ferret, and general staver-off of headaches. At Caravan Tours, the Syrian owner, Mr Leon Kazakian, spoke French and had a sound nose for business. It was no time to slam the door in tourists' faces: he also guessed we would far rather look at palm-trees than gallows.

A fellow-traveller with a grey beard addressed us in perfect French. He was Father Legrand, a missionary from Bangalore, returning to France by easy stages. We liked his smile and the continual merriment in his eyes and he took to us as well. We decided we should travel together. The Syrian rented us a gleaming lemon Land-Rover with the words 'Caravan Tours' painted on it in huge black letters. The driver was a splendid figure, with a square jaw, bright eyes and a jaunty gait. He wore a dashing Prince-of-Wales-check suit and, in a stage whisper, he told us he was an Assyrian and a Nestorian, which was a formidable combination. Assyrians came swarming down from south-eastern Turkey at the beginning of World War I to escape massacre by the Turks. Nostorius was the Syrian-born Patriarch of Constantinople, who, in the early fifth century, taught that the human nature of Christ was separate from His divine nature: a dogma condemned as heretical by the Second Council of Ephesus. Nestorianism, which gained support in northern Syria, was banned throughout the Empire and flourished only in Persia and Mesopotamia.

A number of Nestorian communities who retired into the mountains of Kurdistan were described by Mr Siuffi, French consul in Mosul in 1880, as 'bellicose . . . leading a very frugal life . . . almost wholly independent. Their Patriarch, the Bar Chaman, is supposed to be the lawful successor to St Peter . . . There are a hundred thousand of them in the mountains'. Another consul, M. Pognon, describes in his memoirs how the office of Patriarch had been handed down from eldest son to eldest son in direct line of succession from Nestorius himself. 'Some Patriarchs have been boys of twelve and the present one (1890) is a confirmed drunkard.'

Our Assyrian was called Andy. He was delighted that we knew something of his ancestry, and with fatherly concern he took the three of us across a flat, fertile landscape lined and chequered with irrigation canals, aubergine and cucumber plantations, and forests of date-palms pierced with shafts of light. We passed villages of thatch-roofed mud huts where the long abayas of the women stood out sharply against the sepia soil. Men puffed gently at their hookahs, in the shade outside the Moorish cafés. We came at last to the high arch at Ctesiphon's remains of the second-century Partian palace. The architectural mystery of that massive arch, boldly silhouetted against the sky as if hollowed out by a giant bulldozer, with its faded, variegated bricks, remains unsolved. When the Parthian kingdom was at its height, the entire *iwan* – the great hall of the palace – was covered with a carpet a hundred and sixty feet long, depicting landscapes and rivers and wild animals in gold and precious stones. The Arabs invading Ctesiphon in 637 cut the priceless carpet, distributing the fragments among their troops in lieu of back pay. It took a thousand camels to remove the priceless haul.

I was impelled to Ur by the magic of the name and the silence of the ruins of a civilization which flourished six thousand years ago. Ariane and Father Legrand agreed but curiously Caravan Tours did not. The argument dragged on in oriental style for forty-eight hours. Mr Kazakian advised us to take the night train, then he changed his mind.

'In the days of the British,' he said, 'you could hire a private carriage with cook and manservant. But today the night train is far too dirty and overcrowded.'

In the afternoon it appeared that the night train had been withdrawn, owing to the Tigris having burst its banks and the tracks being flooded. We were to take the day train after all. These were some kind of 'pyjama-floods', to be put on at night and taken off in the morning! Mr Kazakian did not like my humour which, I'm afraid, gets one nowhere in Iraq. Now both day and night trains were plagued to the most amazing degree by dirt, accidents and overcrowding. I said we'd go by car. But the Babylon road was waterlogged like the railway lines: and the Kut road farther to the east, running alongside the bed of the Shatt-el-Ghanat, a tributary of the Tigris, was unnegotiable as well.

O.K., we'd take the day train.

Now Andy the Assyrian and his employer muttered together

in Arabic, and Kazakian had a quick word with two men who had listened to it all. They were detectives, and Kazakian was asking permission. He returned, having changed his mind again. The train was now too tiring and Andy would drive us after all.

My personal 'shadow' glanced at his watch and made an entry in his notebook. Seated at the next table, he had twisted and turned so much the day before to keep an eye on me that his green jacket had become badly rumpled. I waved to him, which startled him, and he gave me a stiff, embarrassed nod. I stopped at a display-board covered with crude caricatures of alleged Israeli atrocities, where Dayan, Golda Meir and Israeli paratroops came in for pretty savage treatment. They had shocks of hair and monstrous noses, like the caricatures the Germans put out during the Occupation. The Arabs, with their neatly combed hair and delicate features, looked more like stunted Swedes. I smiled again at my *alter ego* beside me, and this time he smiled back and deep yellow lines spread across his face, But I still felt uneasy, not with the fear of an air-raid or a skidding car, but with a quiet, continuous apprehension.

Ariane and I found a pale, lonely, rather depressed visitor waiting for us. He was the French Economic Attaché to the Middle East. Moussa was with him and we went into the bar. The barman kept his eye upon us, and we got even closer attention from a sinister pair at the next table. They sipped soda-water and strained for every word. We weren't decrying the government. Indeed, the country was in sound economic health despite the lack of industrialization and the problems of the land-reform programme, for the royalties paid by the oil companies provided eighty percent of the national income and ninety per cent of the budget.

During the First World War, the oil-fields became a new Eldorado and British policy in the area changed. The British got their hands on the southern parts of Syria and Mesopotamia which became Iraq and on Baghdad and Basra.

Despite objections from Colonel Lawrence, Britain let France occupy the greater part of Syria and also Mosul in northern Mesopotamia. Whitehall was disinclined to have borders close to Russia, but changed its mind about the oilfields around Mosul, and when Clemenceau tamely retroceded Mosul to the British he remarked, 'When I want oil, I go down to the shop for it.'

The nice little man from the Quai d'Orsay was stiff and correct, with his neat hair, neat tie, neat jacket, dressed for the morning plane to London. But he thawed at our expatriate informality and spoke of the doubts which the great international companies had. For all the wealth in their oil-fields they were wary of investment, the Baathist government bred insecurity. The Iraq Petroleum Company (I.P.C.), in which Shell, B.P., and the Compagnie Française des Pétroles each had shares was refusing to invest another penny in Iraq, which needed the large oil royalties, for its agriculture was in a bad way. From the thirteenth century until a few years ago, all land was owned by the sheikhs. The British who occupied Iraq between 1920 and 1932 allowed them their prerogatives, so that the existing subdivision of the land would impede the growth of national feeling and delay demands for independence.

The land reform programme following the revolution of 1958 abolished feudal ownership, giving the peasants the land they had previously worked for the sheikhs, but only 3,930,000 acres, a sixth of the national area, was being cultivated. With proper irrigation and scientific farming this could be doubled. Today's farmers, alas, were very poor and even less able than the sheikhs to afford seeds and tools, nor was there a single chemical-fertilizer factory. So the great bare plain, fertile enough if given half a chance, was starving under the swing-plough and human manure the skinny breasts of Asian agriculture. Peasants who could escape rural illiteracy hurried off to the cities for skilled jobs, higher wages and easier living.

North of Baghdad, we passed a low, brick prison-building, surrounded by high walls and guarded by tanks and soldiers clutching sub-machine-guns. Beyond, the Tigris rose smooth between the palm groves and the desert. At intervals along the excellent straight road were low, astonishingly elegant brick-works, with battlements and trefoil arches and tall chimneys plummeting smoke into the sapphire sky. 'A smoking minaret!' Ariane exclaimed, cheerful in the early morning. They were also like saharian fortresses and medieval caravanserai.

The countryside became flat and the soil fertile: a river or irrigation canal was not far away. On the horizon were palm-trees, and, nearer, some of the wheat and barley-fields were under water. We were approaching the much talked-of floods.

Every six miles or so, there was a simple hut manned by two soldiers and a civilian, sitting outside nursing sub-machine-guns and chatting incessantly. Andy told us that the civilian was a spy, and every one of the 'spies' greeted him as an old friend and waved the Land-Rover through.

Several times cars passed with white wooden boxes on their roofs. The long boxes were covered with reddish veils flapping in the breeze, and often wobbly motor-coaches full of shiny faces followed the cars. Andy explained that these were funerals of Shia Moslems bound for the burial-places of the sacred city of Nadjef, south of Baghdad. The bodies would be buried in a simple linen cloth and the coffins brought back for future use. Ariane and Father Legrand would cross themselves or not, depending on the direction of the passing cars, but as neither was too clear where Nadjef lay, they would, half the time, be blessing empty boxes.

The Shute schism put an end to Moslem unity. It generates deep feeling even today and dates from the death of the second Caliph Omar, the ninth century founder of the first Moslem state. Some Moslems wanted Ali as Mahommed's successor. He was a proud, courageous, clever mystic and the Prophet's cousin by birth and son by marriage. His supporters called themselves *chiat Ali* (followers of Ali), a phrase contracted over the centuries to *Shiite*. Others believed that a caliph should be elected democratically to hold office as *primus inter pares*. Adhering to

this orthodox teaching of the Sunna, they became known as Sunnites. The rift developed in appalling massacres and bloody
assassinations, beginning with Ali himself, who was treacherously
slain on his way to the mosque. The legend says that his body was
rolled in a carpet attached to a riderless camel, and that during
the night his ghost took the reins and brought the camel to Nadjef, where his remains are still venerated.

The sects live peacefully together today. The Shiites are fewer,
a million and a half compared to two million Sunnites, but they
call the tune in modern Iraq.

Over the yellow sand rises a minaret with a winding ramp, like
a fair ground helterskelter. Around it a group of women were
gossiping, shrouded in their black *abayas*. It is all that remains
of the ninth century Abbasside mosque. The ascent was easy,
but Andy held my arm closely, brushing against me as the ramp
narrowed. Was he a gigolo for lonely lady-tourists, or a man on
the make? Or maybe he had vertigo?

His 'spies' had disappeared, and we were stopped at every
checkpoint on the journey back. The soldiers stared, confused,
at our passports, but relaxed and smiled pleasantly when Andy
explained that we were French. They were thoroughly likeable
young men with thin moustaches and smiling brown eyes. Here
was another facet of truth in the grim, cruel reality of Iraq.

The village was blinded with sun. Not a café was open, and
nothing was moving on the long main street, except a few women
in their flat slippers, flapping like penguins on the hot asphalt,
and a row of turbaned men squatting against the white walls and
blinking into space. A yellow dog barked against the grip of the
drawn-out midday siesta.

Stopping briefly in Baghdad, we were off again south to Babylon,
through an immense terracotta plain where fields became fewer
and mean flocks of brown-coated sheep munched the sparse
thorns. The acrid dust worked into one's hair, clothes, hands.
Checkpoint followed checkpoint. At Hilla petrol was forty cen-

times a litre! In the repair-shop, black with oil and piled high with old tyres, a garage-hand covered in tar served us from an ancient, creaking hand-pump. Hilla was a large market-town, prosperous and tidy where fruit, corn-cobs and tinned food were sold, and where some of the white foursquare houses had affluent wrought-iron balconies, a sign of unusual wealth.

Four miles on was a large enamelled signpost much like those at home: but this one did not say 'Pontoise' or 'Créteil'. In white against the blue background was the legendary name 'Babylon!'

The site is a majestic, fawn-coloured plain spreading to the horizon, fractured by some cosmic collapse and eroded by the tireless desert wind. There is little left, but how rich and evocative are the age-old bricks stacked either side of the great Processional Avenue! The vanished city of splendour, wealth and refinement becomes peopled with warriors in their gold-plated chariots, and with bejewelled women, their breasts thrusting at fine muslin.

The great age of Babylon was the eighteenth century B.C. under Hammurabi, who gave the city a comprehensive code providing for every public or private eventuality in the life of freeman or slave.

The Iraqi government has plans to rebuild Babylon. This ambitious and arguably futile project is to be financed by Unesco and the Guggenheim Foundation, but is there any point in reconstructing the bare, lifeless bones of the place as they were at the height of its fame? I would sooner walk quietly while the scene and the imagination resurrect the world buried underfoot.

Away to the right, only a flat brick-roof in a state of complete collapse marks the site of the Hanging Gardens, one of the seven wonders of the ancient world; where tropical trees, musky odours and blazing flowers made a luxuriant paradise of what is now ochre dust. Mesopotamia was then a fertile land, criss-crossed with irrigation canals using waters drawn from the Tigris and the Euphrates.

In a gentle breeze, we walked among the quivering memories of these time-defeated walls, past the gate of the mother-goddess Ishtar or Astarte, the goddess of life and fertility, one of the nine gates in the city. Only a single monumental stump, a hundred and fifty feet across, every part decorated with white bulls and dragons with serpents' heads, shows how the images once stood out in relief from the ultramarine glazing on the baked bricks. The glazing has gone but the animals are still there, coloured like the mellow brickwork.

Dead civilizations are a wonder and a despair, particularly here where one of the oldest and most radiant is just dust in a violent, dictatorial land ruled by a bevy of generals. Does civilization come quietly to fruition in places unaccountably suited to it, or does it burst in a shower of sparks, detonated by unknown elements, only to fizzle out like this? I began to weary of this drab, touchy, prying, disbelieving country, and felt an urge to be away from bricks and dust, from foul-smelling men and black-swathed women and the endless pale brown of everything.

Then there was Ur. Father Legrand, in grey flannels and a khaki shirt, his beard blowing about, was in a seventh heaven appropriate to his calling. Ariane was delighted to be away from her researches, and I was eager for the archaeological shrine as I settled back in my seat, arranging my usual cargo of miracle-bottles and scented handkerchiefs. Only Andy seemed cast down, worrying perhaps about this mysterious road to Kut which nobody seemed ever to have used and which the *Guide Bleu* dismissed with contempt.

Again there was unalleviated flatness, with a few wheat and barley-fields, but plenty of thick sheep and scraggy cows, black goats with hair trailing to the ground, and dromedaries breaking the distant pink sky.

A peasant in a spotless turban was a stab of blue at the heart of a cornfield. This is a fertile clay region, with irrigation-canals, ponds, pools and reservoirs fed from the flowing Tigris. There are dark, restful palm-groves, where the peasant women's bright blue and red-violet robes on the ochre earth recall India. We passed a line of women in black, carrying loads on their heads, balancing their burden with both hands and yet keeping their *abayas* in place. Like great birds with half-spread wings, they seemed ready to fly off. One, with her arm curved like a bow, held her bundle in a vivid violet shawl.

The road was excellent, and soon we reached the concrete houses and wide thoroughfares on the outskirts of Kut. The trim green approaches of a spacious modern textile factory contrasted with the drab khaki bricks of so much else. As we neared the town centre, however, the streets narrowed into puddled alleys lined with shabby stalls crudely covered with corrugated iron or cardboard. Bricks are the sign of wealth, and stone has never been used in Iraq and does not even exist, but the vast clay *puszta* is a natural source of bricks. In the main square, verminous old women sold verminous hens and sniggered at me, making the witches of *Macbeth* look like angels of light, while reeking, ragged males crowded round stalls of sweet oranges and juicy dates.

A tyre burst. We were stranded by a pond shimmering like silver in a flat expanse of nothing. Our cavorting Don Juan was revealed as a helpless fumbler. We did what we could to help as yellow lorries passed without stopping. They were full of Bulgarian workmen hired to build the road, which seemed to suggest that there *was* no road. At last, an ancient lorry stopped and the driver helped us, quickly finishing the job, screwing the bolts back into place and refusing a tip.

The suggestion was right. The road gave out and there was nothing ahead but dust and a corrugated-iron track. We shut the windows, sweating as if we were in a yellow steam-room. The dust got in everywhere, in thick layers on our clothes and faces, with the acrid, unmistakable smell of Iraq. We approached Shatra by night, and soldiers guarding a narrow bridge examined our passports by torchlight as Andy thrashed things out with them in Arabic. Neither they nor the people staring spellbound at the yellow Land-Rover were able to agree about the distance between Shatra and Nasiriya, which the British called Ur Junction and where we were to spend the night. Estimates ranged from two to twenty-five miles: arms were extended confidently to various points of the compass including north and east, which was straight into Iran. At last Andy announced Nasiriya was just across the bridge. A lone woman dressed in black, her head held high under a heavy load, passed swift and light as if her feet were winged. Never did I see so light a step – music, a gift of God, pure beauty, already vanished.

At last came Nasiriya, and again the broad thoroughfares leading to a huge main square with tall, mean street-lamps and a confusion of signposts. A low, shabby building called itself a rest-house. But we were too tired to argue and even more so when a scruffy proprietor told us our rooms were let to 'Chikis' (Czech engineers). He pointed unsteadily at the far bank of the black Tigris, where we found a bungalow of sorts, with iron beds too dingy to examine closely, but a bathroom. Not exactly the Ritz! The bath-mat appeared to be retired after a lifetime as a door-mat; the bath was coated with antique filth, and unknown hairs stuck to the wash-basin and the dark grey towel. But there were sweet-scented rose bushes in the garden, and croaking frogs by the pond.

We ate what was left of the food prepared for the 'Chikis' at the 'rest-house'. During the slow service and the awful cooking we argued with Andy, who adamantly refused to take us to the marshes south of Ur, near the Iranian border where Kazakian had said we could go. Few travellers had been there. One of them, Wilfred Thesiger, the best kind of eccentric Englishman, had spent several years there, getting to know the people who were the heroes of his book *The Arabs of the Marshes*. He minutely describes their frugal lives, their warm friendship and unshakeable sense of honour. They had refused the disruption of time. I had set my heart on going to the marshes and I intended to have my way. Ariane took a strong line with Andy, but he wouldn't budge. I urged him more gently, and he gave in. Father Legrand thought we could not depend on his change of heart. All this worried me, but, back in my room, I was more concerned with a well-fed cockroach holding its private Olympics on my pillow.

Next morning we were skidding on the soft sand back on the pitted track with its intermittent pools and tufts of dry gorse. Only a few palm-groves and Bedouins on their sturdy little chestnut horses broke the flat emptiness. And then we saw the huge, truncated pyramid of greyish bricks against the hard sky. It was restored, but still a thrilling sight in these desolate wastes. It was our destination, the great *ziggurat* of Ur.

It was Sir Leonard Woolley who opened the dig for the British Museum. This brilliant archaeologist was originally sent to the Hittite city of Kharkemish in the north of the country, where he was succeeded by Colonel Lawrence, who first appears keeping one eye on the Hittites and a sharper eye on the German engineers building the Berlin-Baghdad railway.

Sir Leonard, who excavated at Ur from 1923 until 1934, claims that the *ziggurat* or temple tower was three storeys high and surmounted by the temple itself. It was the sacred shrine in the twenty-fourth century B.C., during the great period of the third dynasty of Ur. Outside-staircases once wound around the tower. Although today the three storeys and the temple and the staircases have vanished, the huge square base remains. Two hundred feet by two hundred feet, it looks like a truncated trapezium of crude clay-bricks which were left to dry in the sun and which have turned light gold after three thousand, four hundred years.

We were stopped by an elderly guard, armed and brandishing a rifle; his black robe was held by a cartridge belt, his face was as lined as old leather and his dark eyes were blazing. My *salam alekum* earned us a surprisingly tender smile which revealed black stumps of teeth. He spoke in utterly fragmented English and told us he had worked with 'Mr Woolley'. He knew, he said, all there was to know about the site, and he had himself found donkey-tracks and the impression of chariot-wheels in the royal cemetery. Below the *ziggurat* was the deserted and abandoned dig, with brick walls where a number of sanctuaries had stood, including the temple dedicated to the god Nannar. Successively destroyed and rebuilt under the Sumerians and Akkadians, ravaged by the Elamites, the walls were restored by the Kassites, only to fall into the hands of Nebuchadnezzar II. I understood little of those bygone religions in which the god Nannar sailed the sky in a rowing boat.

Down a flinty path were the royal tombs, and we stooped into a grotto hollowed out in the side of the plateau. We crawled along a hot, dusty, claustrophobic passage-way and came out into a second, smaller grotto. These dark, gaping caverns had served as burial places for the third dynasty monarchs who ruled Ur from 2184 until 2015 B.C. Buried with them were their wives, favourites, servant-girls, soldiers, domestic animals, donkeys and horses harnessed to chariots of gold, with their treasures of jewels, gold plates and musical instruments like the three harps in the Baghdad Museum, each inlaid with gold and precious woods. The rulers and their dutiful attendants were buried in the grottoes, while the passages yielded the priceless objects in the same museum. In *Excavations at Ur,* Sir Leonard Woolley tells how, in one of the tombs, were the remains of a score of servant-girls, each wearing a gold headband. Concluding that they had been obliged to take their own lives when their lord died, he noticed that one had her head-band still clutched in her hand as if summoned at short notice: a youthful, affecting touch which brings close the last moments of a girl snatched cruelly from life four thousand years ago.

The side of a ravine about twelve feet across and a hundred feet deep looks like a colossal slab of Neapolitan ice-cream. It is the famous Flood Wall, where each layer corresponds to a different geological period and where the time of the Flood is clearly marked by a belt of yellow clay. At the top of the Flood Wall, Woolley found bituminous remains with the impression of a basket identical with the wicker baskets used today to collect bitumen for lighting huts and caulking fishing-boats.

Ur is an ultimate isolation of space and time, beyond history and archaeology, filled with an arid sense of the infinity of things.

I left the walls of the Sumerian and Akkadian city behind and ambled up a twisting lane leant against a derelict brick wall and, glancing over it, I saw a fire-place at the far end of a room covered with a flat roof. Our escort tapped me with his rifle-butt and pointed at a brick. It bore a simple inscription, 'Abraham's House'.

The lane was deserted, but I could imagine the donkey, the child, the woman in black and the turbaned man appearing around the corner, just as they would have looked to Abraham three thousand years ago. I laid my hand gently on the ruined wall, humble remains of the ancient splendour. It needs no marble palaces to transmit life over centuries. This wall, this lane, these fading wheel-tracks, or the atmosphere and the horizon, can restore a vanished world.

On our way back to the Land-Rover, behind the *ziggurat,* the guard disappeared. He turned up again with a leather-bound volume, green with age. The Visitors' book! It was late April and we were the first visitors this year. Three had come last year. We shook hands heartily with this somewhat lonely man.

'Salam,' he said 'Salam. Marhaba. Goodbye.'

Andy drove us to the marshes without further quibbling. It was market-day in the muddy, over-crowded village of Souk-el-Chouyouk, with hunks of mutton, rank-smelling fish, egg-plants, corn-cobs, oranges, dates, and great clouds of buzzing flies. We were stopped by a man in a lounge suit who climbed in without a by-your-leave, pushing Ariane along the seat and ordering us to the far end of a courtyard where machine-guns prickled from the roof. We realized that we had been carted off to jail. Two men with rifles yelled us out of the car and across a yard crowded with soldiers, police plain-clothes officials, and men in *arabayas* and turbans who followed us with intense curiosity. Foreigners are rare, and my trousers added spice to the event.

We were led into a large room before the hostile scrutiny of a man behind a huge desk. His suit was black, his tie was black, his moustache was black. He indicated that we should sit on benches by the wall. I sat facing my companions, while a succession of plain-clothes officers strode in and out. The chief of police questioned Andy, and when Ariane asked him what on earth was going on, he snapped at her rudely. Where was the attentive chauffeur, the foppish, posturing lady-killer? Our passports were examined. They wrote down our names, dates of birth, and professions. Father Legrand inspired confidence, but they were suspicious of Ariane, though her passport said she was an agricultural engineer. My own passport had vanished. I treated the chief to my best smile. 'What is the purpose of your visit?' he barked. 'I am a tourist,' I said, 'anxious not to miss Ur and the Marshes.' But tourism sounded like a cheap alibi in a developing country with a spy fixation.

As time dragged by, Ariane became impatient and raised her voice, bringing a herd of plain-clothes men down on us. I told her in private slang to shut up, which she did. The flies buzzed. It was hot and a bit scarey. This bloodthirsty crew could lock us up indefinitely in heaven knows what kind of cells. Would the ambassador succeed in getting us out? Wisest perhaps to look calm and confident. I let out a sigh as casually as I could. Ariane had become silent and a little pale. Father Legrand seemed cheerful and unruffled. Andy sat with his head in his hand, refusing to translate the most harmless questions. I dozed off, and reopened my eyes three hours later, just as the chief of police was returning our passports to Andy. 'This gentleman,' said Andy, 'has kindly agreed to accompany us on our journey through the marshes.' Well, why not? He could act as a guide while he kept an eye on us. The orderly presented arms. It was all over.

Later in Baghdad we learned about border-fighting with Iran over the ill-defined territorial waters of the Shatt el Arab. Perhaps we were mistaken for Iranian spies.

We followed a canal through the dusty *puszta*. The sky was

lead-dark, the air was close and wet, and the marshes glistened in the shade of the palms. We passed lock-gates where bare-legged men were casting big nets or hauling them in, full of silvery fish. Long, black, slim boats, tapered like gondolas, rustled over the water, caulked with bitumen, as they always have been. The smiling fishermen surged forward to greet the deputy. Ariane was in the crowd, shaking hands all round. 'Mafish fish?' she asked and the deputy roared with laughter at her awful mixture of Arabic and English. The houses, known as *mudhifs,* are domo-roofed and built of layered reeds and mud. The walls and ceilings are supported by pillars made of tightly-tied bundles of reeds. Stouter reeds, a lattice-work for the lower parts of the walls, in normal weather these keep cool, and let the water out when it floods.

The deputy sprawled comfortably in the front seat. I was in the back, wedged tight between my two companions while we giggled like school-children. Suddenly I realized that he was asking something. He wanted to know what we thought of the Palestinian issue. It was an insidious question, for, although Iraq makes warlike noises, she has never lent tangible support to the Palestinian cause, nor has she been slow to jail the Feda-yeens (though perhaps for their own protection). The Baathist government regard them as trouble-makers, to be soft-soaped in public but stamped on in private. The Palestinians feel, and not without good reason, that it will be a long time before Iraq, like Saudi Arabia and other neighbouring countries, risks a single life against the Jewish enemy.

'We don't know much about it,' we replied, wise as serpents. 'What matters, surely, is that peace should somehow be pre-served.'

'When you get back to France,' said the deputy, 'you must tell your readers* that the Arabs have justice on their side and that, if the French government has any sense, it will adhere to the policy laid down by General de Gaulle.'

While we remained evasively thick-headed, our double-dealing

* Ouch! In Iraq as in Syria, journalist = spy.

Andy claimed that he was watering down the deputy's remarks, but I imagine his English just wasn't good enough to cope with the original version.

We stopped outside a perfect reed-built house showing up gold against a smooth green rice-field. Foreigners, Andy maintained, were not allowed to stop, to go into houses, to talk to people, or to photograph them. I resorted to deaf-and-dumb language with the deputy, indicating I wanted to use my camera. He willingly agreed. The householder was a noble-looking, tall, fine-featured man, with almost black skin. His short white robe hung loosely, Indian-style, leaving his legs bare, and he wore a thick spotless turban. He owned a cow with a splendid glossy coat, which grazed placidly beside us. He ushered us into his pillared, latticed *mudhif* to introduce us to his wife, a beautiful, bare-headed, dark girl with an Indo-European look emphasized by a brown garment, a cross between *abaya* and sari.

At the next village we were sipping hot lemon tea from tiny glasses when the village schoolmaster came over and introduced himself. He had a young, open face, wore European clothes and talked broken English. He spoke enthusiastically about his job. Soon afterwards we were joined by three other men, including a policeman who behaved very obsequiously to the deputy. One after another, they paid for a round of tea. They were a friendly group and told us, with Andy's help, how important it was that the people stand by de Gaulle's policy. The deputy was greeted with tremendous respect everywhere. One old and heavily wrinkled peasant even went so far as to kiss his hand. The children thronged round him, laughing. He had been quite pleasant to us and obviously had a way with people.

We wanted to see more of the marshes. 'It would have been a long way to come just for a week-end.' Father Legrand thought this the wittiest remark he had ever heard. Dear man, he made a wonderful audience! We had only to open our lips and he began to shake with mirth.

Ariane, who was looking after public relations for the expedition, went to talk to some people in the doorway of a *mudhif*.

Between the palm-trees I could see her red shirt bobbing up and down as she bowed to each of them, like a well-trained geisha girl. The deputy was highly amused. Andy sulked.

The owner of the *mudhif* was short and stocky and deeply lined, and his short blue *arabaya* revealed powerfully muscled legs. His wife was delightfully young and pretty. Her childlike hands emerged from her black *abaya* and closed on a ball of dough. She kneaded it, flattened it, and pressed it to the burning wall of a clay oven shaped like a scooped-out egg. Several fish were hanging to dry from a rope stretched between two palm-trees, and beyond was an older, still beautiful woman watching us quietly. The first wife, maybe? She had a blue tattoo-mark on her chin. Two houses were set at right-angles. One contained the bedroom, where the big brass bed had a flower-patterned cotton counterpane and a neat pile of blankets and pillows. Aluminium kitchen utensils and earthenware plates and dishes were set out on a wooden table together with a large black transistor radio brightly embellished with nickel. The floor was covered with a woollen carpet, and the whole place was meticulously clean and tidy, with an unexpected hint of something close to affluence. In the second house the mothers were using their fingers to eat from aluminium plates. A pair of fish hung drying from the wall in a corner of the room. The women stood up and smiled at us – or perhaps their greeting was solely for their lord and master, who laughed and jested without pause, obviously a bright spark. His wives didn't take their eyes off him, trying to anticipate his every wish. Their farewells were heartfelt and energetic: *Marhaba-Shoucrane* ('Goodbye – Thank you'). until I was quite out of breath from shaking hands. The deputy was overjoyed. Andy looked stunned and incredulous.

During the drive back, the deputy questioned Andy, and with the string of proper names in his answers ('Yes, I'm an Assyrian ... that's right, a Nestorian ... I work as a guide for Caravan Tours'), I almost believed I could understand Arabic. The deputy gave him a telephone number to ring if he returned, and reminded us how popular the French are and how willingly we had been trusted. 'We would never have allowed British or American people to enter the Marshland or set foot inside the houses,' he added. Very big of you, Mr Deputy!

Andy drove like a maniac all the way home, choking us with dust, and making the shock-absorbers groan and crick my spine. He jammed on the brakes under the nostrils of a cow standing in the way and eyeing him with deserved contempt. He tried to overtake enormous lorries, did not succeed, sounded his horn and flew into a tantrum. I hid my face in horror. The coach and lorry-drivers – the only drivers one ever sees on Iraqi roads – drove with great wariness and propriety, always pulling over and waving us through.

At last an asphalt road relieved my afflicted back. Kut, repulsive enough, appeared like a metropolis compared to Shatra, where the battery gave out. A mechanic covered in grease poked at it with a couple of sticks and it started again. Although grateful, we decided we still ought to find a garage, and drove over a bridge and up the muddy main street until we came to a wooden hut piled high with worn-out tyres. The car was soon surrounded by a dense crowd, and I watched through the dust-caked windscreen with fascination as two pairs of brown arms busied themselves with pliers probing, jerking, thrusting each other aside, wavering, pliers held high, and then plunging back into the engine. I kept my fingers crossed as I hoped we would not have to spend the night in Shatra. Children, wide-eyed with curiosity, clustered like flies, and one little girl in black, her eyes pale grey as a mountain lake, held up her small brother with motherly concern. She stared intently at me and flitted away through the filth, a frail, dancing little shadow who would grow up and grow old and die in the same foul village. I watched her, this Tanagra figurine with the sky-clear eyes, until she disappeared down another mud-strewn alley. Among the ragged, snotty bunch of urchins, one boy, who edged quite close, wore a white shirt and a surprisingly clean pair of shorts. He spoke a few words of broken English, revelling in his scholarship, and turned quite pink when I complimented him. One fair child contrasted oddly with the others. The crusaders did not come this far, except for the Children's Crusade of 1212, when the pious merchants of Marseilles sold thirty thousand waifs to the pirates of Algiers for the slave-markets of Alexandria and Baghdad. Was the girl descended from a Frankish prisoner snatched by a raiding-party to be a slave at some emir's court, or from a beautiful captive in a sultan's harem, or was she (less romantically perhaps) the offspring of an ephemeral union between a British soldier and a local girl?

I took pictures of them all and they laughed and shrieked with excitement, jostling for places 'Thank you, thank you!' they shouted, trooping after the car.

In the filthy shops the foodstuffs gave off such a horrible smell that it was a miracle that cholera had not struck the whole region.

The régime claims credit for a major reform in the field of primary education. All children living in towns are now supposed to receive a proper education, and all the boys in rural areas get schooling, but only two per cent of the girls. English is a compulsory second language from primary school onwards. Everywhere I went I saw children hanging about the streets in what were surely school hours, and the only child I ever heard speak English was the little boy in Shatra. But a significant start has been made.

A massive herd of grey buffaloes thundered across the road. The traffic, mainly lorries and small buses, is not dense; but the drivers don't consider a dog worth braking for, and along the road are the bodies of saluki-like dogs with long black-and-white coats. The dog is an impure animal to Moslems and his name is a violent term of abuse. The deputy had been vastly amused to hear me curse the driver of a lorry which blinded me with dust: *'Kalb benkalb!'* ('Dog! Son of a dog!') I couldn't curse now, even in jest. I drooped in my seat, tired at the end of a long day, idly watching the deep violet hue of the desert skyline. We were going to lose Father Legrand, who had been so patient with our whims and shifts of mood.

The Baghdad Palace seemed genuinely palatial; the secret police were like old friends; and my bath promised byzantine delights.

Jacques de Favières, the French Cultural attaché, is the most brilliant of guides, a man bewitched by Baghdad. He took us to the great Shiite mosque at Khadimain. Two tanks stood outside the Ministry of Information, presumably guaranteeing the free flow of information. General Bakr should know how insecure Iraqi governments are and how near conspiracy always lies. Public opinion has never played much part in the displacement of one régime by another; indeed it is often confused, lukewarm or non-existent. Public opinion did not intervene for the Hashemites whom Britain set on the throne, nor did it save Nuri-as-Said when he tried to escape, disguised as an Arab woman; he was recognized, tortured, drawn and quartered by order of General Kassem. General Bakr, his successor, is a loutish, grim-eyed figure with a low forehead and the inevitable black moustache. His portrait hangs on the walls of all public and official buildings. He gives the impression of being the mouthpiece of a collective leadership rather than an independent head. The real 'strong man' of the régime appears to be Maddam Hussein, a ruthless character who once attempted to murder Kassem.

In contrast to the publicity given to its executions, Baghdad largely glossed over the bloody war against the Kurds. No one got to hear that the Iraqi army used napalm on a Kurdish village. And yet there are thirteen million Kurds in Iran, Turkey, Syria and even Russia. About three million of them live in the woods and mountains of northern Iraq. Their existence is meagre. There are no roads, and their purchasing power is minimal. Middle-class citizens of Baghdad prefer to buy from Syria or the Lebanon. The Kurdish revolt was essentially economic. Mustafa Barzani, Kassem's comrade-in-arms during the 1958 revolution, talked the new government into recognizing the Democratic Party of Unified Kurdistan, of which he was leader. He set himself up as head of the Kurdish nationalist movement and in 1961 started

an armed revolt. After subjecting his people to eight years of
war and misery, he responded to secret overtures from Baghdad.
He always avoided making the government lose face and even
declared that the Kurds 'are loyal patriots' and advocated 'co-
operation between the Kurdish party and the Arab-Socialist Baath
party'. An agreement was drawn up by the cabinet minister
Abdel Rahman Bazzaz on 29 June 1966 but only ratified by the
government in January 1970. By then poor Bazzaz had been
languishing in an Iraqi jail for some time. Undaunted by charges
of political opportunism, and anxious to rid himself of some
extremists, General Bakr tried forty-four Iraqi army officers who
had been pacifying Kurdistan and all forty-four were found
guilty and sentenced to death – an expeditious way of dealing
with people insufficiently adept at political trimming.

The Iraqi government has been reluctant to carry out the cen-
sus provided for in the agreement of March 1970 to determine
the areas of Kurdish habitation as a preliminary to autonomy.
Instead, the Bakr régime and the Christian religious authorities
are persuading Moslems and Christians to settle in Kirkuk, a
rich oil area in northern Iraq. If an Arab majority can be established there, it will remain in Iraq's jurisdiction. The situation
drags on, and the only group to benefit are members of the regular army whose high rates of pay and benefits make them the new
mandarins, a class apart, rife with corruption and nepotism.

The magnificent mosque at Khadimain, with its golden domes,
was restored in the nineteenth century by a Shah of Persia, and
Persian influence is reflected in the four pointed minarets and
the colourful mosaics covering the whole interior. Only the faithful can enter the building, but since no doors in Iraq are closed
to Favières, we were soon standing by the tomb of the Shiite
*immams* venerated there. Light reflects continuously from the
stalactite vaulting covering the ceiling, and the mosque blazes
with rich colours. It is like stepping into the pages of the *Arabian
Nights*. As we made our way slowly around the tomb, we were
preceded and followed by ten or so Shiites who gave us very

black looks. There were no other Europeans about, and I was the only woman in the building. The Shiites are the Jansenists, the untouchables, the *hassidim* of Islam who insist on strict observance of the law. They wait for the coming of the *immam* Kashi, who, unlike the Messiah, will not redeem them until mankind has redeemed itself through virtue.

Men and women strolled and chatted in the blue and gold courtyard. The surrounding streets are muddy and animated, with booths, selling food and fabrics, set in the walls of the old Turkish houses, whose unscathed *moucharabies* and wooden-balustraded balconies look out to a small three-cornered square now threatened under the city-development plans. Shiite delegates were doing their best to preserve these relics but their views carry little weight.

Two eighteenth-century mosques sprout beside the chestnut Tigris; their brick minarets have grown slightly askew as if mimicking the Tower of Pisa, and the glazed tiles on their cross-pieces lend bright touches of turquoise and ultramarine to the dull landscape. The Tigris often invades the powdery soil and, as there are no stones to shore up river-banks, again and again it imperils these frail historic buildings.

The indefatigable Favières led us up dizzy stairs to the top of the minaret of the ninety-fifth honeycombed mosque we had visited that day. I felt I was scaling the north face of a ball-point pen. The tower stood at the far end of a cemetery overlooking the old Baghdad of the Caliphs, stiletto-like minarets thrust into the hazy sky. A little grey donkey trotted below us. Ariane, who had no head for heights, waited for us in the cemetery. For me a touch of dizziness was the lesser of two evils, as the dead had been wrapped in winding-sheets and placed, coffinless, in shallow ditches with only a single layer of bricks and a shovelful of dusty earth and a sour, pungent smell hung over the place, fraught with the threat of pestilence. Children shrilled at us for 'Baksheesh! Baksheesh!' and young men in shirt-sleeves sauntered around, cheerful, friendly, inquisitive. Three women sat dry-eyed on a tombstone, emitting loud, incisive wails, and their strange dirge followed us together with the rank, oppressive odour.

There seem to be as many mosques in Baghdad as there are churches in Rome, and I was not sorry to return to the city-centre and the ultra-modern banks and the other glass-and-concrete buildings.

I once saw the Chief Rabbi of Baghdad interviewed on French television. He was a rather pathetic old man with a myopic stare and a quavery voice. He claimed that Iraqi Jews were well-treated and free to do exactly as they chose; they didn't want to go and live in Israel. These answers struck me as readily predictable but the interview left me sceptical. I was eager to see the Jewish quarter for myself.

The Jews of Iraq claim direct descent from Israelites whom Nebuchadnezzar carried into captivity in the sixth century B.C. The Koran prohibits Moslems from handling money on a professional basis, and this gave the Jews undisputed supremacy as bankers and changers. Their wealth and influence consequently incurred the hostility of their fellow-citizens. In Byzantine times, the caliphs granted them financial autonomy and placed their trust in them, as they suspected the Christians of spying for Byzantium. The city became the chief financial market of the eastern Mediterranean. This position lasted until the nineteenth century, when suddenly the wind of favour changed. A scion of the well-to-do Sassoon family spent several weeks in the caliph's jails before he escaped to India. There, amassing a huge fortune, he founded a dynasty which presided over the financial life of British India and concessionist Shanghai, before he moved to London and continued his remarkable career as a British citizen.

Towards the end of the nineteenth century the Universal Jewish Alliance, under the presidency of the Austrian banker, Baron Hirsch, came to the rescue of tens of thousands who had been unable or unwilling to leave the country.

The Hashemite kings never discriminated against the Jews.

The idyll ended, however, in 1941 when Hadj Amine-el-Husseini, Grand Mufti of Jerusalem, began to propagate Hitler's theories in the Middle East. The Jews began to be ill-treated as early as 1934 and the first pogroms were in 1941.

Serious emigration of the Jews did not begin until 1949, when the Communist leaders were hanged in public and a considerable number of Jews were arrested.

This once-prosperous community of over a quarter of a million has dwindled to about five thousand. After the Six-Day War the frontiers were closed to the survivors and they lost their basic freedoms, like the right to live where they chose or to practise a trade or profession, own a telephone, or venture beyond rigid boundaries. It is hard to reconcile these facts with the words of Mr Bitterlin, Secretary-General of the Franco-Arab Solidarity Association. Writing in the 'Libres Opinions' column of *Le Monde* on 8–9 February 1970, he said he would not go so far as to say that Iraqi Jews live like French Jews but 'although the situation may from time to time have been difficult for Jews living in Arab countries, it has improved – especially in Iraq . . . where Iraqis of Jewish extraction lead normal working lives and are perfectly free to practise their religion'. He added imperturbably, 'The possessions of Jews who have left Iraq since 1948 have been placed in sequestration, and the state has undertaken to hand them back if their owners return.' Did he seriously think that the Iraqi exchequer would be swamped with claims? He went on to say (and this is undeniably true) that the rise of Zionism had often caused despondency among Jews living in Arab countries. 'Many have left; others have stayed put and incurred suspicion because of Israel's attempt to make martyrs of them.' This attempt, if real, has been fairly enthusiastically abetted by some of the Arab states.

Now Favières was to take us to the ghetto of the Iraqi Jews. We turned off a main thoroughfare into a badly rutted alley oozing filth through every crevice. I was up to my ankles in mud. We passed a ruined synagogue where the house next door had been blown up: the large central patio was surrounded by a crumbling colonnade with a ruined gallery, and rats scuttled about the courtyard. 'Try not to stare,' said Favières. 'We aren't really allowed here.'

The people walked past us in silence, but a number of young schoolgirls stared at us, looking neat in their black smocks and white collars. In their big, dark, eyes, there was a fearful curiosity. The atmosphere was one of ruin unchecked and of things falling apart. Outside a school, a plaque which had once borne the name of a Jewish benefactor was covered over with Arabic. At every turn were closed shops, empty offices, illegible names and soundless shadows. Cooped up in the same ghetto in bizarre juxtaposition with these Jews were Palestinian refugees, the heroic brother Arabs whose cause was trumpeted in propaganda broadcasts, but who got no military support and, when they arrived, were dumped in this revolting cesspool, where their faces soon took on the scared and harassed look of their detested foes and neighbours. They were even lucky, for often refugees were jailed for trivial offences, and torture was common for those who pressed for even the smallest political independence.

When the Civil War broke out in Jordan in 1969 the Iraqi units stationed there did not intervene and were promptly re-called, leaving their 'fedayeen brothers' to fend for themselves.

How could one like Iraq? The filth, the ignorance lie like a cloud over the children's smiles, the physical beauty, the nobility of the desert, the archaeological treasures, and everything else that might otherwise give pleasure; it was all too sad, too sick. I was glad to leave, and I have no desire to return, in spite of Khorsabad and Mosul, and in spite of a compelling curiosity to see beyond the hills.

# The Lebanon

BEIRUT airport was in darkness as the Air France Boeing touched down on the only lighted runway. On our right was a dismal pile of smoking debris, all that remained of a Lebanese International Airways Liner. Beyond it was a single charred wing and burnt-out shell of part of the fleet of Middle East Airlines. Israeli commandos had coolly landed here the day before in French-built Hirondelle helicopters, and the remnants of their visit were already stacked out of sight at the far end of the airfield. The night air was mild, scented; airport staff flitted like ghosts, and passengers dispersed silently in the terminal buildings, which at any other time would have echoed with shouts and laughter and loud-speaker messages. Today you could cut the atmosphere with a knife, and the customs men, usually so smiling, were tense and withdrawn. Beyond the glass partition separating travellers from the public were only a few harassed, uneasy figures, and the glass itself was pierced by the star-shaped holes of two warning shots. My friend Guy Abela clasped me like a sister returned from the brink of disaster. 'Spineless devils,' he spat, 'without guts enough to fire a single shot!' This anger was aimed at the Lebanese airport police, one of whom had given an Israeli paratrooper a coin for the Coca-Cola machine so that he could calmly quench his thirst.

The French press had described the situation as 'explosive', and my family had begged me so strenuously not to leave that I now had an absurd sense of stepping heroically into a lion's den. I had decided on a grave face and to take care to do nothing to disturb my Lebanese friends.

I was three hours from a November-grey Paris, where passengers for Beirut had soon packed into Hall thirty-three with passengers for the El Al flight to Tel-Aviv. Officialdom clearly had a keener interest in geography than in current affairs, and we were a mixed bag of Semites. The confrontation passed off serenely, and the 'rival' groups offered quick smiles in an atmosphere of complicity.

Beirut, under a starry sky, stretched along the sea, waste patches intermixed with piles of Manhattan-style neon signs, cinemas and restaurants. Beirut glittered; but only two limousines were outside the Caves du Roi. The Hotel Phoenicia is enormous, with braided, bustling page-boys, and a lobby as big as a ballroom. The young men at the reception desk were undeniably efficient. My room was lovely, with a view over the sea. It had everything I could possibly need: matches, sewing-kit, a bowl of fruit. Highly-polished luxury fills me with a timeless sense of enjoyment, and I bathed while the maid ironed my dresses. The moon shimmered on the bay, and the mountain rose in the distant darkness.

The smell of the sea and the clear morning light put a spring in my step as I passed the big hotels on the Esplanade des Français. I lingered in the sun at rich displays of antiques or oriental arts and crafts. Friendly taxis honked insistently when they drew level with me. The United States Embassy, flanked with palm-trees, was shielded by a cordon of armed troops. It had become a favourite target for the ever-increasing demonstrations staged by Lebanese and Palestinian students. The Lebanon was one of the very few places where Palestinians lived without fear of arrest or massacres. They were demonstrating their claim to a national existence and more often than not, their left-wing views. Their influence at the Lebanese university and the powerful and wealthy American University was such that it angered the Moslem and Christian business communities, and was beginning to alarm the government who began to employ stricter measures against them.

We were at Raucheh, a residential neighbourhood of luxury flats. Beyond was a series of modern hotels, numberless appalling concrete cubes.

The sun blazed, and the beaches (already covered with oil and seaweed) had acquired the litter of prefabricated 'beach-houses' for the capital's bourgeoisie. Finally we came to the super-smart Plage Saint-Simon, where Guy Abéla had his chalet. All my Lebanese friends were there, and the atmosphere was gay and unrestrained. How had I arrived, they asked. 'By helicopter,' I replied, forgetting my resolution to be careful. My dubious joke made them laugh even louder. Guy Abéla was about forty, a saturnine man with a dumpy frame and large head tilted to one side. His brown hair was brushed straight back and streaked with white. He studied me silently. An expression of gloom behind his spectacles gave way so often to a surprisingly youthful smile. He was of a breed of 'drawing-room guerrillas' that flourished in Beirut. The more active guerrillas of Al Fatah took up a large part of his dreams, if not of his huge house. His bedroom was on the scale of a Gothic cathedral, and all the magic smells of the east wafted from a host of glittering cut-glass bottles in his scarcely less spacious bathroom. But he spent the greater part of his time in the library with its dark panel-work and rich bindings, surrounded by the loving care of his mother and aunts, stout oriental ladies prattling in Arabic and gorging themselves on cakes dripping with honey.

The talk was of Lebanese International Airways, whose fleet of six tolerably ancient machines had been destroyed on the ground. The company had already brought itself to the brink of bankruptcy; the Israelis had completed its misfortunes. 'Poor May,' they sighed, commiserating lightly with the owner's wife.

A businessman introduced a note of mischief, telling us that L.I.A. and M.E.A., the other Lebanese airlines, were insured with Lloyd's of London and could expect compensation to the tune of twenty million pounds, the full market rate for brand-new air-craft. L.I.A. would do really rather well out of the operation.

'Knowing you Lebanese,' I said, 'I wonder you didn't dress up and launch the attack yourselves.'

'Now, why didn't we think of that?' they exclaimed.

The same businessman loosed a second shaft by telling us that many of the companies with whom Lloyd's themselves were insured were financed from Jewish sources: at least two per cent were Israeli-owned. My friends loved this information. Guy had to take off his glasses and wipe the lenses. So much for the chastened mood I had expected to find! Jean Eddé described his encounter in the bar of the Hotel Saint-Georges,* with Emir Megid, patriarch of the frontier village of Megidieh. The poor emir had suffered a terrible blow. Finding that the Lebanese guerrillas had camped and revictualled in the village, the Israelis had retaliated by doing the same. The losses sustained during the operation included twenty-four broken windows and fifty-two heads of cattle, including the prize bull which, with stupendous energy, had supplied the needs of every cow in Megidieh. The emir had been obliged to pay compensation all round.

The laughter continued while the massive red sun sank into the green sea, sending the only shiver through this hedonistic, insulated, nineteenth-century world.

None of the promised New Year festivities had been cancelled, and we found ourselves in the home of a fashionable Egyptian playboy, winsome and dashing in spite of his fifty years. He was one of those refugees from the Nasser régime who, although thoroughly welcomed in Beirut, looked down on his Lebanese hosts as bumpkins and tradespeople. The bay-windows of his apartment looked over a city ablaze with neon lights. Pretty women pressed close to men in impeccable dinner jackets. The music was sweet and raucous by turns, and punctuated by snatches of Italian, English, French and German. Ribbentrop, son of Hitler's minister for foreign affairs, was swaying his hips and

* One of Beirut's main centres of conversation.

*Above* Jerash — the Gerasa
of Alexander the Great —
where the huge oval forum
is ringed with Roman
colonnades and paved with
its original flagstones

*Right* Along the narrow
defile to Petra, a high wall of
red rocks, fantastic and
oppressive, weighed down
on shivering Ariane . . .

*Above* We passed from one valley to another, human travellers in a desert desolation, our guides, Ariane, and the author at the end of the overwhelmed caravan

*Left* A peasant woman, fine-featured and unveiled, squatting with her baby beside her, displays Nabataean terracotta cups, vases and larmiers

The author endeavouring to ride a desert-policeman's camel in the desert of Wadi-Ram. In the background, Moses, the driver

In the streets of Baghdad, women and children selling flat loaves of bread

*Above* At Samarra, a group of women, watching over a few skinny cows, were gossiping shrouded in their black *abayas*

*Left* Over the yellow sands, rises a minaret with a winding ramp, like a helter-skelter from a fairground; the remains of a ninth century Abbaside mosque: Samarra

jerking his arms convulsively. Surrounded by these frolics, the French ambassador, friendly but doleful, brooded on the end of an era. 'The Lebanon will never be the same again!' Samer, handsome, dark-lidded and my favourite 'drawing-room guerrilla', threaded his feline way towards me, and at every step there were coos from enraptured ladies. He told me confidentially that he had just returned from Cairo 'as a mark of solidarity'. 'I saw some fedayeen while I was there,' he added. He whispered like a conspirator, his voice soft as velvet. He was delightful, intolerant, languid, finicky, slothful but sensitive, warm-hearted and . . . admiring. I teased him about the palatial residence he lived in all alone, and he deafened me with theories which made Dr Habache's seem tepid. Had it ever struck him, I asked, that his house would make a marvellous refugee camp for two hundred displaced Palestinians? And he threw back his head and laughed aloud.

At three in the morning, the car bogged down in a traffic jam on the Esplanade de Raucheh, and grinning youths pelted us with streamers and paper missiles. Friendly, high-spirited, with paper hats and cardboard trumpets, they spun round and round in the light of the headlamps. They were Moslems, but Beirut is Beirut and they were seeing in the New Year.

Next morning, the country's leading French-language newspaper reported that the Minister of the Interior made a special visit to the airport and swigged champagne with the staff to thank them for their heroism in the treacherous enemy attack.

The silvery Koura plain was a vast olive-grove even in biblical times, and our car twisted gently up the rocky foothills to the home of Georges Borgi, an enthralling lecturer and a fount of archaeological knowledge. Short and dark with eyes like a gazelle, he appeared buried so deep in his chair that I felt he half-hoped never to move from it.

He lives in the small market-town of Amoun, where austere, elegant Turkish houses cling to the mountain-side. His own house is very large and stands apart from the others. A stout little lady in black had welcomed us warmly, and behind her, hanging back, were Borgi's two married sisters, both markedly respectful to their brother. We drank coffee in the unheated drawing-room, seated on gilded chairs. The reverence for Borgi from the female members of the household was extended to me, and they kept offering me chocolates, with that charming, generous, oriental persistence that plays havoc with the French liver. Borgi accepted the idolatrous admiration with the dignity of Saladin receiving some newly subjugated sheikh.

A Cistercian abbey-fortress perching on a nearby mountain-top had been restored by a beguiling Austrian ambassador, Beycha-Wauthier. It was called Deir Balamand or Belmont by the Crusaders who crowned so many of these hills with cloisters and strongholds.

From a cliff overhanging the deep, precipitous valley of Kadisha, the rock-face appears riddled with grottoes and bristling monasteries, ancient havens for the Maronite Christians dispersed by the Arab invasions in the seventh century. Shunning the dead towns of Syria, they found impregnable hide-outs in these parts. The monasteries were not abandoned until the nineteenth century, and even today there are still a few hermits living in the grottoes. The town of Diman, close by Kadisha, is still the patriarchal see of the Maronite faith.

We stopped to take a respectful look at the seven last cedars of Lebanon, a scene which prompted Lamartine to reflect, as usual, that *'tout est dépeuplé'*. A thousand years before Christ the whole region was overgrown with cedars. They were felled by the Phoenicians, cut into segments and masts, logs and planks, and sold to the woodless Pharaohs for their weight in gold.

The sheer-faced mountains gave way to placid snow-capped hills like camels' humps. The Cedars is the much-vaunted winter resort which tugs the imagination on bleak November days in London or Paris with posters proclaiming: 'Ski at eleven, lie on a beach at twelve. Enjoy sun, sea and snow all day, every day.'

The Qualaat Sanjil or Saint-Gilles Castle in Tripoli was built seven and a half centuries ago by Raymond of Saint-Gilles, Count of Toulouse. A highly-strung southerner, cowardly and courageous by turns, despite these vacillations he gave ample evidence of ardent faith and total dedication to the Crusade. He did not live to see Tripoli achieve fame and prosperity when, after his death, it became renowned throughout Palestine for its schools of medicine and philosophy, its glass-blowers and silk-mercers and a soft fabric made from camel's hair.

The collapse of the kingdom of Jerusalem brought swift and startling changes. Every Frankish fortress within the county of Tripoli and the principality of Antioch fell to the Mamelukes, and Tripoli was itself wrested from young Bohemond VI. Both sides were briefly united to repel the Mongol invaders. Tripoli suffered little and the Moslem population received lands from the sultan, including the area at the foot of the Qalaat Sanjil for an Arab town – which is the site of Tripoli today.

The streets are cut with trenches for water mains, and the markets stink of rancid oil. But here and there is a pretty door or a graceful façade, with a wrought-iron balcony or a pediment engraved with Arabic characters over the entrance to a *Medresseh* or Koranic school. The handsome, light-coloured mosques, their squat domes over-hanging curved niches, are often built with the stones from ruined crusader churches.

Modern Tripoli is ugly, but it is very much alive and growing. There are earthworks and building-sites and an oil refinery, for this is the end of the pipeline* which runs through Jordan from Saudi Arabia. The city teems with Palestinian refugees and political agitation. Its quivering vitality echoes its Greek and Roman past, Byzantine rule, Arab conquest, and the days of the valiant Saint-Gilles.

The road to Byblos stretches between the hills and the sea. Traffic is heavy and the drivers edge forward, blazing their horns. At one end of the bay in a sudden deep cleft is the rock Nahr-el-Kalb, the Dog's Nose, where every invader from Nebu-chadnezzar to Gouraud, has carved his inscription. The mists

---

* Owned by the Tapline company.

of history drift away in this defile, where the Babylonians halted and the Persians, Greeks, Romans, Arabs, crusaders, Turks and, more recently, the French paused to nest, lulled perhaps by the gentle beauty of the bay, like a shell around the humble fishing-village of Beirut.

There is a Saint-Tropez Inn in Byblos, as there is a Hotel Byblos in Saint-Tropez. On this mild winter Sunday we ate the exquisite *mésés,* a mysterious local hors d'oeuvres, all the colours of a Saint-Laurent collection while, beyond the terrace, the little yellow port rocked with single-masted green *tartans.*

The ancient Byblos, known as Gebal to the Phoenicians and as Gibelet to the crusaders, overlooks the sea. A stone sea-anchor lies among the obelisks, the *bet-els* sacred to the Phoenicians, and mauve anemones push up through the soft grass. The tomb of the Phoenician King Hiram, who married his daughter to the great King David in the eleventh century B.C., rises, spare and simple, in a delicate light, shaded by much-photographed fig-trees.

The archaeologist Dunant, who opened up the dig, made a trench through the layers of stone surviving from the Phoenician, Persian, Achaean, Hellenistic and, finally, Roman walls. One can identify the different periods by the distinctive cut of the stones, but my attention wandered to the little medieval church of St John, rising in the distance.

Invasion after invasion, siege after siege, races conquering and dying, and nothing now but these ruins, serene and golden in the setting sun, and the keeper waiting for his baksheesh and a yellow dog gazing at us with large, damp eyes.

Bab-ad-Driss is Beirut's main shopping-street, old-fashioned, full of noisy traffic and every kind of merchandise. The market stalls are a riot of grapefruits, oranges, lemons, limes, strawberries, apples, grapes, olives, vegetables, corn-cobs, flowers, fruits and vegetables from the coastal plain between Saida and the Israeli frontier, together with cereals from the Bekka plain to the north of Beirut. The farms are mostly small and medium-sized holdings, and their yield only feeds a third of the population. The Lebanon, often mountainous, always hilly, is dry, and there is little irrigation. The country sometimes appears lush but only twenty-seven per cent is cultivated. Perhaps forty per cent could be worked with profit.

The Lebanon is poor and emigration is high. The population is about two million, but there are a million and a half Lebanese scattered across the world. The dispersion began about two centuries ago. As with the Jewish diaspora, the people spread towards the wealthier countries: the United States, Canada, South America and, more recently, Australia and New Zealand. Some Lebanese have left for the French-speaking countries of Black Africa, Saudi Arabia, and the Trucial States.

The country's wealth is not from agriculture. The Lebanon acts as banker and forwarding agent for neighbouring Arab countries, and ships vast quantities of oil from her sea-ports at Beirut and Tripoli. Her lucrative pre-eminence is already threatened by the rapid modernization of Syria, where the ports of Latakia and Tartus are linked by road, rail and pipeline to the oil-fields of Karkemish and North Rumeila.

Otherwise the country's income is from industry, mostly small concerns like the 1,600 firms specializing in canned foods, oil, beer and textiles, and the growing tourist trade, and money sent home from the Lebanese living abroad.

Serious thoughts just slip away in Bab-ad-Driss, as they do elsewhere in this buoyant country.

Most men dress in suits. Some older ones wear the fez adopted during the Turkish occupation. An occasional peasant from the Bekka plain, the two mountain masses, wears the long striped *abaya*. The women are lightly dressed: the old wear black *abayas* and some are veiled.

In contrast, the nearby Jewish quarter was very still, with many shutters pulled to, and the streets empty except for an occasional car or bicycle and a very few pedestrians. Some good-humoured Lebanese troops were on guard, apparently to protect the Jews in case of a Palestinian attack. Lebanese Jews are not persecuted at all; indeed they are totally assimilated and enjoy full civil rights. A few Sephardic families still speak Ladino,* a thirteenth century Spanish, blended with Arabic and sprinkled with Turkish. Some make a modest living from the ancient craft of *passementerie*. Others are everywhere in the community: bankers, such as the Zilkas, stockbrokers, traders, money-changers, journalists, musicians.

Relations between the communities are courteous and lack friction, though their private lives rarely overlap. I saw no Jewish guest at the parties I attended in Beirut. Michel Eddé, a lawyer who has a number of Jewish clients, seemed quite taken aback when I asked if they ever came to his home. He told me never, though sometimes he might lunch with them.

On another tack, I discovered the world of antique dealers, with the expert guidance of my Gascon-pro-Arab friend, Jacques de Sirlan, who lives overlooking the sea, surrounded by his own fabulous collection. Here, Odile, his vivacious wife, plied me with coffee while I sat enthralled by his passionate enthusiasm. Or we would pay other visits to a labyrinth of antique-dealers. Each time it would be coffee and cigarettes and conversation was light and brisk with plenty of banter, and a slight suggestion that we were partners in some conspiracy. The dealer would disappear and bring us special items. Jacques would whisper advice, pointing out a fake, noting a bronze engraving or the relief-work on a statuette, or the shape of a piece of pottery.

Beirut is the main market for Syrian and Jordanian antiques, and Syria has many highly-skilled forgers whose wares are dumped in Beirut or sent through Jordan to Tel-Aviv to capture cheerful American dollars.

By evening I had acquired the basis of a collection, a headache, a confident feeling that I was half-way to mastering a subject, and the effects of too much coffee.

\* \* \*

* Descended from the European Jews who originally settled in Spain and Portugal. In 1492 there was a mass exodus from the peninsula, precipitated by the persecutions to which the Sephardim were subjected by the Catholic Kings. Sephardic communities were set up all along the Mediterranean coast.

Should I wear this or that? I settled for the low-cut dress and set out for the reception of the Haddad ladies.

The mother and three daughters welcomed their guests. It was a black-tie occasion, and though the women were not very tall, nor very slender, they were very colourful. Their dark, stocky little men appeared to lurk in the folds of the velvet curtains, exchanging hushed words and knowing looks. Was there some plot afoot, or were they just chatting about business and local politics? Our hostess was affecting an interest in archaeology, and assured us that every one of the items displayed in her glass cabinets was at least two thousand years old.

'A likely story!' someone whispered, 'I'm the decorator.'

A white-turbanned army of servants brought on a score of small impeccable tables and a gargantuan buffet: pâtés, smoked salmon, caviare, choice meats. It was worthy of Sardanapalus and vanished as quickly as it had appeared, as did the mountain of cheeses, desserts, gâteaux, compotes, tarts, creams and exotic fruits, and the litres of champagne.

This is Beirut, opulent, sumptuous and scandalous. There is oriental magnificence, unstinting hospitality; the guest is honoured beyond western reason. But this is not a world for reason or for listening; it is a world to enjoy, where events, if they obtrude at all, are so muffled that they lose all effect. A kind of rest-cure to dull anxieties and to obscure problems and pessimism, it is a seductive world, sealed off, protected, in which people live as though the twentieth century had never happened.

The excellent Beirut museum is small, but represents the region from the earliest times. The Phoenicians of the second millennium B.C. are fascinating as a race of traders and seafarers who exported their pottery and glassware and their alphabet throughout the Mediterranean. They may have reached Britain, and (some even say) America. Glittering among the earthenware and wood-carvings was a glass cabinet containing the Golden Warriors, dozens of filiform figurines very much like the statues

of Giacometti. They are bronze and coated with gold. All have
the high, pointed head-dress of the Pharaohs, forerunner of the
Phrygian bonnet worn by ancient fishermen, and the *hennin*
fashionable in the Middle Ages. It is still echoed today in the
coifs wrapped in black or white veils worn by women in the
Lebanese highlands.

By now an accepted disciple, I travelled with Borgi south from
Beirut, through heady jungles of orange trees to the temple of
Echmoun, recently excavated by Dunant. Beneath a low thick
wall of massive stones stands the throne of Astarte, the goddess
of fertility. Its wide, grey stone seat is for ever unoccupied, while
the arm-rests rise on each side in the shape of sphinxes with
spread wings. These sphinxes were inseparable companions of
the goddess, and are said to be the forebears of Cupid and of
the cherubin of the Christian era. Echmoun himself was the god
of healing and renewal, a Phoenician combination of Mercury
and Aesculapius. The temple nestles in a huge orchard of orange
and eucalyptus which, from the top of the wall, looks like a rich
emerald carpet.

Saida, the Sidon of Phoenicia, pushed up its massive Frankish
towers against the grey sea. A wind had risen and rain threatened.
At the end of the mole leading to the castle we hurried down
the worn steps, braced against the wind that whipped the battlements, the parapet and our faces. God knows I love those profli-
gate crusaders, by turn warriors and diplomats, swords in one
hand, missals in the other; but their fortresses are better at a
distance. Their romantic appeal dwindles close to. They are so
much alike. They must have frozen, the Therouane family who
had held sway here during the two centuries in which the
Crusaders controlled the region. Such barons assimilated themselves so completely that today you can still find the Arabic forms
of their names like Sanjil (Saint-Gilles) and Balaman (Belmont).

Gradually the crusader-knights and their ladies abandoned
their legs of mutton and haunches of venison and also changed
their fur-cloaks and thick tunics for the local *keffiehs* wrapped

around their helmets as a protection against sandstorms, while *arabayas* kept their armour from overheating. The ladies, just like the wealthy Moslem women, wore long light robes and mantelets embroidered with gold and precious stones. Around them now were Arab servants; their horses were tended by Moslem grooms and their children were brought up by native nurses.

Since the invaders' income derived mainly from taxes levied on merchandise transported overland to the coast, the Moslem traders could count on being well treated and accorded complete freedom of movement. The Templars extended their banking facilities to Arab customers, and members of the Order became experts in Moslem affairs. They hunted together, and even in war they lavished gallant and chivalrous gestures on one another.

Friendship thus established, love was quick to follow, and the Patriarch of Jerusalem solemnized a series of mixed marriages from which sprang generations of fair-haired, blue-eyed Orientals. For instance, in 1098, Baldwin, the brother of Godfrey of Bouillon and later king of Jerusalem, treacherously secured control of the Principality of Antioch and married Princess Arda, daughter of Thoros, Armenian lord of Taurus, thus gaining support of the large and prosperous Armenian population and becoming a great king of Jerusalem. A generation later, Baldwin II married Morphia, an Armenian princess. His mighty vassal, Jocelin of Courthenay, married the sister of Thoros, king of Rupenia. These examples were followed wholesale by other men. The conflict between Saladin and the grotesque, muddle-headed Guy of Lusignan dragged on for two years, but the soldiers habitually sang and danced together as soon as the day's fighting was over as well as when Frankish soldiers married Arab women. Saladin's men deserted for the smiling eyes of a Frankish camp-follower. The Franks saw that, to keep the political pendulum swinging their way, they must exploit divisions between the Moslem princes and this complicated game was not confused by religious fanaticism. Just as the Templars protected the pilgrims on the road to Mecca, the Bedouins were concerned for the safety of St Catherine's monastery in Sinaï and of the devotees who journeyed to it. But, alas, this restrained, tolerant and thoroughly oriental attitude suffered from the later arrivals from Europe. Prince Usama of Shaizai was praying in the ancient El Aqsa mosque as a guest of the Templars, when a baron recently arrived in the Holy Land provoked him rudely. A Templar appeared and begged the Arab to dismiss the outburst as the error of a European as yet unshorn of his barbarous ways. As well as bringing grim fortresses and blue eyes to these shores, these ruffians, saints, plunderers, romantics and sages filled the misty medieval world with dreams of chivalry, colour and romance, dreams of the 'Land beyond the Seas'.

Saida has forty thousand inhabitants, and the inevitable piles of concrete with peeling paintwork, and washing at every window. But the arches and alleys of old Saida are the Lebanon of countless prints. Peasants with soiled turbans urge small grey donkeys with raucous cries, the animals all but hidden under burdens so large that they block the narrow streets. A young man in a threadbare jacket sat picking his nose beneath a grinning portrait of Nasser; all around, traders dealt in corn, fruit, old clothes, even books. It began to rain and was soon muddy underfoot; our clothes were splattered. An icy wind caught us in a small square where a small mosque was topped by two white cupolas. The inside was modest, simple, moving, a place for prayer. A little wearily we continued our afternoon tour of Saida, followed by shrill, thin music from cafés where men puffed idly at gurgling hookahs and Nasser's portrait grinned from every shadowy booth.

Under Syrian rule, in the seventeenth century, Saida was the principal port of Damascus. Fakhr-ed-Din, who built it, was of Frankish blood and gave special protection to the French. Later it passed into the hands of the Hospitallers.

The Hospitallers, like the Templars, were a curious religious-military order dedicated to dispensing charity and doing battle for Christ. In 1040, a pious burgher from Amalfi first opened a hospice for poor pilgrims with the blessing of the Egyptian government. The monks acknowledged only the authority of the Pope. In 1118, the hospice introduced an order for knights who would be bound by the triple vow of poverty, chastity and obedience and dedicated to combating the infidel. The Order was called 'Hospitallers of the Temple' or Templars. By the end of the twelfth century the military Orders dominated the church and were the biggest landowners in the Holy Land. They wielded political power because of the shortage of troops there, though there were heavy loses among the knights who 'took the cross', who were unfamiliar with Arab tactics and became easy victims of malaria or dysentery. At first the Orders only policed the bandit-infested roads, but soon they supplied the king with a force of seasoned, dedicated warriors who cost him nothing and were, indeed, wealthy enough to build and maintain fortresses such as few nobles could afford. They were shrewd administrators, who superintended any county or principality left in the hands of a widow or orphan.

Their numbers were small but battles could be won or lost by a hundred horsemen and a thousand foot-soldiers.

With their immense wealth they became local bankers to the king and the Holy See, and later to Moslems and Christians living in the area. From this position they could threaten or usurp the king's authority. The Templars boycotted the Egyptian expedition of 1158, although the Hospitallers played an active part in it. Keen rivalry had developed between the two Orders, and they seldom fought side by side. Each would conclude agreements with some of the most fanatic sects such as the Assassins, in clear defiance of the royal will.

Already a threat to royal authority in the East, they became a threat to the king in France as well, and in the fourteenth century they fell foul of King Philippe IV, who gave them no quarter; his enmity cost them their property and often their lives.

Chastened, the Hospitallers sought a quieter life: for a while they took shelter on Rhodes; and in the sixteenth century they moved to Valletta, to found the order of the Knights of Malta.

Young boys played football or stood talking in groups around
our car. I wondered about the thoughts and dreams of a young
person living in Saida, what fired him, gave him strength. For
some it would be Al Fatah. There were fifteen thousand Palestinian refugees, living in all the rebelliousness, agitation, wild
talk, propaganda, hidden arms, nationalist aspirations, poverty,
despair, all the dissension of a refugee-camp. To a young Arab,
Al Fatah often meant more than a bourgeois Palestinian revolutionary party: it meant freedom fighters, heroes, glory and
dreams of Arab unity.

Borgi shrugged at these thoughts. For him the only realities
were at least three thousand years old. I reminded him of the
'Romanized' Jewish historian, Flavius Josephus, who wrote of
Alexander's plan to use Syrian mercenaries, which cost him the
support of the Jewish troops, because Syrians, in spite of their
eagerness, simply would not fight with or against Jews. Hopes
of unity in the Middle East seem as unfulfilled today as in those
early times when Jews and Syrians were but small, semi-nomadic
tribes herding their sheep across hills and plains.

'Early times?' said Borgi, 'the Roman period is not early. It
is late!'

A bistro beside the little harbour was fussily tricked out with
cowherds' stools and fishing-nets, and run by a man who had
spent some time in Mexico but had little to show for it but his
nickname, Pépé. His fish smelt odd and his coffee was watery.
We were very soon back on the coastal road to Tyre. Ancient
Tyre was a flourishing seaport deriving a vast income from the
trading-posts which its wealthy ship-owners and intrepid sailors
set up throughout the Mediterranean. Traces of their enterprise are found far beyond Gibraltar, as far as the Hebrides and
perhaps even Maryland. Tyre's wealth was a tempting target for
the less prosperous in the seventh century B.C. Nebuchadnezzar
attacked it pitilessly, as Alexander did three centuries later. It
was an island then, and held out against the Macedonian for
three years but in the end he built a jetty between the island
and the coast, thereby cutting it off and starving it into submis-

sion. Strangely, archaeologists have not found the smallest Phoenician potsherd there, nor a fragment of Greek inscription. 'Only Roman stuff,' sighed Borgi, in obvious disgust at the magnificent columns, the broad avenues, and the necropolis where excavation was in progress; the stone sarcophagi stacked like concrete slabs on a building site. Emir Chehab, the oddest Lebanese successor to men like Dunant and Seyrig, had managed to uncover the hippodrome as a majestic expanse of sand which retained several of its tiered rows of seats.

The village of Sour, its milky beach, scattered with seaweed and a few old huts and half a dozen *tartans,* looking like a typical small fishing-harbour, is all that remains of the ancient metropolis, the great Phoenician port, mother of the Hellenistic arts and sciences, the mighty Frankish fortified city. Sandstorms have erased its former grandeur less cruelly than history.

We returned by a mountain-route through woods of pine and oak, deserted except for a few peasant women in long, bright skirts and strange, truncated head-dresses, urging small, silky grey donkeys. We stopped briefly at Beit-ed-Din, a small Arab palace built in the last century.

For a few miles through these rugged, fragrant highlands we were far away from dapper little Lebanon, which craves for *la belle vie* so intensely that nothing is serious and the death of a soldier or a fedayeen is merely wearisome.

All Beirut attended an evening lecture on the Phoenicians, amid the usual greetings, smiles and gossip. A crowd clustered around the French ambassador, and Guy Abéla introduced a whole stream of guests, including a lawyer named Camille Aboussouan, who claims to own the most comprehensive library in the Middle East and considers himself a notable thinker.

'A truthful book about the Arabs,' he said, 'would never see the light of day.'

I expressed surprise at this pronouncement.

'The entire French publishing trade is in the hands of the Jews.'

I had never thought of Robert Laffont, Bernard Privat, Roland Landenbach as a bunch of rabid Zionists.

'And what about Ania Franco's publishers? Were they asleep when they bought *Les Palestiniens*.'

'It gladdens my heart,' he rolled on, 'that since 1967 there has emerged a movement in the European capitals so powerful that before long there will be genocide on a Hitlerian scale and we shall see the Israeli Jews driven into the sea.'

My caviare sandwich stuck in my throat. I turned away without answering.

'The man is gaga,' Guy whispered. 'I can't tell you how it riles me to hear people talk like that. Offensive rubbish helps no one. Why doesn't he do something useful, like helping Al Fatah?'

Any cause, however worthy, is tarnished by the raving of men like Aboussouan where sterile violence only wearies the listener. Shukery, the first leader of Al Fatah, had shown all too clearly the back-lash of wild and empty rhetoric.

The evening continued at Michel el Khoury's. 'Sheikh Michel', as he is called, is the son of Bechara el Khoury, a former president and the brother of Khalil, lawyer and one-time Minister of Social Affairs. Family links of this kind are commonplace in the Lebanon. The political cake is shared out among relations, and many receive more than one slice; it is not unusual for a minister to hold three or four portfolios. Nearly all Lebanese politicians, whether the best of friends or the worst of enemies, are almost certainly kinsmen. The political parties and the major cities are in the hands of a few powerful dynasties. The political cake is also divided, on a reasonably fair basis, among the various religious faiths. Parliamentary seats and government posts are allotted in proportion to the size of each community. The same system operates in the civil service, especially at the top, where the Sunnites (though fewer in number) are in a more commanding position than the Shiites. There is an unwritten law that the president should be Maronite, the prime minister Sunnite, and the speaker Shiite.

My host and his fine, sensitive wife lived in a large house on one of the city's hilltops, surrounded by pretty, foursquare Turkish houses with lancet windows and Roman-tiled roofs.

A Lollobrigidesque Italian archaeologist was talking to the wife of the O.R.T.F. correspondent, Mme Andrieux, a little woman with grey hair and a peremptory tone. There was a Lebanese playwright, a painter, a sprinkling of wives, and Michel Eddé, one-time Minister of Information, and now the life and soul of the party. Amid roars of laughter, he told us how the Ministers of Information of the various Arab governments had met in Bizerta a few years earlier; how in the preceding weeks he had prepared a weighty report, fully expecting, not unreasonably, that the first day of the conference would be for serious deliberation. However, they had gone to Carthage on a sightseeing tour followed by a siesta and a ball at the Pardo. The following day came and went, and no one ever heard the report, which stayed in his brief-case. They did actually meet, waving to each other from a distance to avoid any possible dispute. The agenda had finally called for the odd half-hour of work, when the representatives of the three wealthy nations (Saudi Arabia, Kuwait and Iraq) pulled long faces while the rest, poor relations, beamed in anticipation.

He quoted one exchange between the haves and the have-nots:

At this point I should like to pay tribute to the kindness, generosity and magnanimity of Saudi Arabia . . .

(Interrupting, deeply embarrassed):

No, no, no, we are neither kind nor generous nor magnanimous. We have had more than enough of paying and paying . . .

But you *are* kind! You really are!

We aren't, I tell you!

(Melodramatically):

Alas, our own situation is as black as our faces . . . !

The rich nations and poor nations could at least share laughter.

I was distracted by snatches of a lively exchange between Mme Andrieux and Michel el Khoury. Khoury was claiming that the Jews had no right to build a state in Palestine. They had left more than two thousand years ago, whereas the Arabs had lived there from time immemorial. But since it was a fact that the Jews *were* in Palestine, I asked him to tell me what he thought should now be done. It was not an Arab concern, he thought. The Great Powers had penalized the Arabs for other people's crimes, and it was iniquitous that the Jews should stay which, of course, they wouldn't, as they would be driven into the sea.

And how was this to be effected? By genocide, apparently. No invader, he claimed, had ever held on to Palestine. The crusaders only lasted two hundred years and nowadays, with everything happening so much faster, Israel would very soon be destroyed.

Mme Andrieux was quite crimson with enthusiasm.

The Israelis, she claimed, were not even entitled to be called Jews, but were a sadistic pack of Nazi storm troopers! Jews were sensitive, cultured, intelligent human beings, many of whom she had met in Paris and some of whom, indeed, were good friends of hers. Khoury was not to be drawn into this argument, considering Jews to be servile or arrogant and it was high time they were all put paid to.

Choking on my silence, I left. The purpose of my journey was to watch, listen and try to understand; I needed to stay and, more important, I very much wanted to come back; no I must hold my tongue. Here were a people, proud in all their lordly poverty, their timeless elegance, their soft songs and shrill tongues. I had the feeling that every moment would be a discovery, a surprise, a delight, an emotion. Life itself seemed to wait around every corner and for this I would swallow my share of affronts.

Time passes, words fade, and today Michel el Khoury favours a settlement with Israel. As for Mme Andrieux, I am mercifully not among her favoured Jewish friends.

A visit to Baalbeck with Georges Borgi restored my peace of mind.

We reached it through the Chtaura pass, which crosses the Lebanon's snow-capped mountains. The wind was ice-cold, and snow clung to tufts of grass beside the road. The mountains were rocky and bare like a series of geometric planes, purple and white against the ultramarine sky, scarred now and then by lines of concrete monsters.

Baalbeck is sixteen hundred feet above sea level, and the wind had turned gusty. The monumental architraves, the sculptures of horses and human figures, the great walls of giant blocks of stone together and against the mountains are awesome, almost oppressive relics of the second-century temple of Jupiter built on the site of the Greek Heliopolis. Even Borgi could forgive Baalbeck for being 'merely Roman'.

After lunch in the Palmyra Hotel, came a brief visit to Anjar. Brief, because Borgi held it in contempt for being only Arabic eighth century A.D. and because the Libyans have been at it. The term 'archaeology' could not be applied to their kind of butchery. The four columns had been raised any-old-how just to impress tourists. And they had made no attempt to document their work. Disgraceful or not, I very much liked those four slender columns standing out against the shifting sky, and Anjar, its ruined vastness crowned by the huge, barren, snow-topped mountains, struck me as very romantic. Fragments of pottery, deep shades of blue with streaks of green and ochre, were irresistibly beautiful, and I just had time to gather a few.

This same funny little country with its two and a half million inhabitants and its fourteen different religious persuasions is a strange microcosm, because on the whole it functions rather well. The balance is precarious. Fifty-three per cent of the population are chiefly Christian, or Maronites, who tend to look down on the Uniate Greeks, although both are attached to Rome and known locally as the R.Rs. (*Rattachés à Rome*). The latter are equally contemptuous of the Christian Greeks and the Orthodox community and give as good as they receive. The Assyro-Chaldaeans and a few Syrian Monophysites are a small minority descended from refugees from the Arab invasions in the seventh century.

The Christians owe a great deal to the French Mandate which gave them protection and brought social development to the Maronites, with excellent French schools and a substantial European market. The Mandate did more for the Armenians who poured into the country between 1920 and 1925, fleeing from the Turkish massacres. Although other Christians, especially Maronites, were hostile to them, fearing their competition as traders and businessmen, the French ensured that they became fully integrated, arguing that their numerical strength and inherent abilities would cement the Christian majority. The Armenian population swelled from fifty thousand to two hundred thousand.

The situation has changed remarkably little since the Crusades. The Frankish kings regarded the Armenian community as a mainstay and often married Armenian girls. They equally relied on the Orthodox community who might butcher the Armenians or be butchered by them, and the Latins looked on in disdain.

Had the Krach des Chevaliers and the surrounding area been incorporated into the Lebanon under the 1920 Mandate, and there were sound geographical and historical reasons why it might have been, the Greek Orthodox community would have been a sizeable majority. The Vatican intervened however; the Krach stayed in Syrian hands and the R.Rs remained the largest religious group. Their high birthrate has kept them their supremacy ever since.

The Moslems are forty-six per cent of the population, and split between the Sunnites and the Shiites, with a sprinkling of Kurds and Ishmaelites. The Druses are a law unto themselves, deriving their beliefs from Zoroastrianism, an abstract religion from the sixth century B.C. Persia, with no priests and no place of worship. They do not bury their dead, but lay them on stones like the Pharsees, who are direct heirs of the Zoroastrians, and left Persia to escape persecution in the sixth century A.D. The head of the Druse community, Kamal Jumblat, is also leader of the Progressive Socialist Party and has established a cemetery for the Druses killed in the uprising of 1958. Like all Druse cemeteries it makes much of the male and female principles of life, the phallus and the egg. Druses were not hellenized by contact with Alexander's armies along the coast between Sidon and Tyre, but moved into the highlands, keeping their distinctive faith and becoming a robust, warlike tribe. One of the teachings of their strange esoteric religion is that they try to deceive non-Druses, and will reveal nothing about their religion save that the sect was born of a Moslem schism in the twelfth century.

Khalil el Khoury, the brother of Michel, my Savonarola-like ex-Minister of Tourism, was thick-skinned, jovial and fair, with mischievous blue eyes: amusing, intelligent, with the thoroughly disabused air of a man who has seen everything at an early age and cannot be taken in. He is the absolute opposite of Michel whose toughness and intransigence I rather like. Michel had told me (rather pathetically, I thought) that he had spent his whole life endeavouring to be as unlike his brother as possible.

Khalil, sensing a good audience, would argue gleefully that since the Lebanese army bore no resemblance to a genuine fighting force, nothing could be more natural than its decision to fire on guerrillas as a means of avoiding a showdown with Israel. The embargo on the sale of arms to the Middle East had been a boon for the Lebanon. When it was lifted they had to take delivery of those wretched six Mirages which they didn't know what to do with. And to pay for them! It wasn't France's fault; it was the villainous Arab League who forced the sale.

He could adopt a different tone of voice, interrupting the deft, bold thrusts of his fork and wringing his podgy hands, demanding to know what the Jews could possibly be after, why would they concentrate their troops along the border? The Lebanese were not a warlike people; they had nothing against Israel; they were just good, quiet, gentle lambs.

These melodramatic protestations are not without a basis in truth. After the State of Israel came into being, the two countries had a tacit desire for mutual co-operation, until the emergence after the Six-Day War of the guerrillas who carried out raids along the Lebanon's southern border, training their mortars night after night on the kibbutzim close to the Golan heights. The two countries are natural extensions one of the other, sharing the same history, the same shores, and the same cultures, whose inhabitants, despite different ethnic origins, have so many characteristics: liveliness of mind, lack of insularity, and an active involvement in the financial and intellectual affairs of the world. On either side of that explosive frontier dwell resourceful highly developed, liberal and unfailingly inquisitive people.

It rained on my last day in the Lebanon. Grey rain and the Mediterranean simply do not work, especially when the newspaper headlines announced: Mock air raid at noon today in Beirut and suburbs. The newspaper was full of useful tips:

1 Remain perfectly cool and calm.
2 Do not loiter or dither.
3 Make for the nearest shelter. (On this occasion you need merely station yourself *beside* the shelter).
4 If at the office, stop work at once and go straight to the shelter.
5 If driving, make for the shelter or take cover in a hole beside the road. In the latter event, lie on your stomach with your hands clasped behind your neck, keeping your elbows pressed to the ground, until the all-clear sounds.

My towering taxi-driver friend, whose heavily scarred face was a memento of his days with the second French Armoured Division, set off for the embassy, promising to take no notice of any mock air-raid, and he was as good as his word. We swept through the pouring rain like his armoured car in the Cyrenaican campaign, shooting vast sprays of water on either side. As the sirens began to wail, he swore vigorously and accelerated. I heard a shrill whistle-blast; the army was on the prowl. 'They'd be better off guarding the refugee camps and keeping the guerrillas out of the country,' he muttered.

At the embassy I drank two glasses of champagne against the

rain. The General Manager of Air-France, who had just returned from New York, was complaining bitterly of the losses on the American route, boycotted by Americans and especially by Jews. Obviously the whole thing was a regrettable mistake, and he seemed vaguely hostile to everything and everyone about him. The United States ambassador, a friendly little man who appeared to speak no French, rested a kindly hand on my shoulder, confiding that there was nothing to choose between the people living in this part of the world; they were all equally worthless. I was still absorbing these sentiments when I was buttonholed by the domineering wife of a superannuated general. 'My dear,' she croaked, 'the unutterable gall of these Jews! There may *just* have been a case for the Six-Day War, but the rest is really too much! Thank heaven a French fleet is on its way! By the way, would you care for a round of golf tomorrow?'

I long to return to my beloved Lebanon with its uninvolved collusiveness, its selfish, hedonistic hospitality, where life is as light as a strip of orange-scented marshmallow.

# Syria

THE road out of the Lebanon follows the low, winding coast. With my Lebanese friends, we were travelling in two cars, which drew up outside a small frontier-post. One driver took our passports, but returned saying that the Syrians wouldn't let us in because Piero Founi's passport gave his occupation as 'Journalist'. The immigration authorities were so excited that they refused to hand back any of our papers until they had looked us over one by one. Michel Eddé, who used to be Minister of Information in the Lebanon, always expressed the view that the Syrians were fools, utterly dim about everything, especially propaganda, at which the Israelis were past masters. He used to tell how after the '67 war he organized a tour of western journalists to the refugee camps and hospitals in Syria, to show them among other things what napalm does to its victims. The Syrians had turned the whole party back at the frontier, and when he telephoned his Syrian opposite number he was told that all journalists were spies. 'A ridiculous objection,' he had countered, 'when the entire Syrian General Staff is on the Israeli payroll!'

A uniformed official studied me, frowning in his effort to establish that I really was the creature portrayed in my passport photograph. I began to have doubts myself. My Lebanese friends showered him with Arabic and his brow smoothed a little, but not much. Lebanese women are sin, Sodom and Gomorrah Incorporated, to a puritanical, Baathist Syrian. We survived the scrutiny, but the Syrians were implacable about Piero Founi, journalist. We wailed, we argued, we entreated; they rang Damascus and Beirut. But it was still no go. JOURNALIST HELD AT FRONTIER. We pondered, conferred, parleyed, made grotesque suggestions, half-witted suggestions, and got nowhere. Guy Abéla decided that we would cross the border at another point, and we doubled back fifty miles and went east, away from the sea to another border post, with the same barricade thrown across the road. This time we stopped some miles from the frontier and Guy selected an enormous tin of Danish ham from our stockpile. Ham seemed curious baksheesh for a Moslem, but Guy had a gleam behind his spectacles. He addressed a few gentle words to a big man in a grey suit, whose eyes lit up at the sight of the Danish ham. He led us into a poky, drab office where we drank the bitterest coffee I have ever tasted. The baksheesh ham lay on the desk, and a slab of chocolate seemed to clinch whatever deal Guy was about.

We drove through plains and low hills of silver olive groves, and rejoined the coast of Latakia, known as Liche in the time of the Franks. The harbour is steadily silting up despite continual dredging, but the city will come to life again when work is completed on the road between Damascus and the Iraqi frontier. It will become a clearing-house for the Syrian and Iraqi products passing through the Lebanon, and for the oil which a new pipeline will bring from North Rumeila in Southern Iraq.

The modern part of the city is well laid-out, with broad thoroughfares and public gardens with plenty of trees, but the usual towering apartments and flapping laundry. There was no shrill haggling or lively gossip, no blaring horns or squealing brakes; the silence was startling, and so was the absence of traffic, with only a few cycles and an occasional car obeying the impassive lights. We stopped in a quiet street to eat our sandwiches and stretch our legs. We laughed and shouted, standing or squatting on the kerb. People stared at us amazed, their eyes condemning our sybaritic way and the capitalist Lebanese opulence of our cars and clothing. A woman of about fifty asked me quietly if I was Lebanese. I told her I was French and she smiled hesitantly. She had known some French people during the Mandate. But she fell silent, and she stared at me, and a sense of unease stirred me. Whatever merit this country might possess, it was not the home of free speech.

Accelerating noisily, we headed north to Ras Shamra, site of the ancient city of Ugarit, where Gabriel Saadeh, a professor of archaeology and a very charming man, was waiting for us. Guy was feeling strained and on edge, and we rushed past the neo-lithic foundations and the remains of the Phoenician walls. Archaeological sites, like Spanish inns, are exhilarating or gloomy, depending on the mood and on memory or imagination. There are no stirring monuments or slender colonnades at Ugarit, only potsherds and broken masonry. I pocketed a few, and found a glassy, chipped stone wich turned out to be a neolithic razor. This chaotic array of fragments marks the first private library in the ancient world. Tablets had been found here, depicting animals and plants. This neolithic site was inhabited in the fifth millennium B.C., and, before the site was discovered, Egyptolo-gists working at Tell-Amarna, capital of the kingdom of Ikhana-ton, were disconcerted to find tablets dating from the fifteenth century B.C. and originating from Ugarit. Writing to Ikhanaton, the reforming monotheist pharaoh and also the husband of the exquisite Nefertiti, the King of Ugarit, like any other humble vassal, sent a tablet saying: 'Lord, I prostrate myself before you and roll myself in the dust like a dog.'

Gabriel Saadeh showed me the site of the tablet-room, and the spot where, in 1955, archaeologists found the table on which a Hittite king of the fourteenth century B.C. had issued the direst threats against the Phoenician city, but which in the event reached its destination after the city had fallen to the Hittites. The prin-cipal industry of Ugarit was the manufacture of purple dye, and the city flourished until the twelfth century B.C. The oldest alphabet originated there, dating from the fifteenth century B.C. and using thirty characters. From it came the Phoenician alphabet, to which the Greeks added the vowels they needed for phonetic purposes. Guy Abéla disagreed emphatically. In his view the oldest known alphabet was the one found at Byblos, as I had been told during my visit to the Lebanese site; but Saadeh insisted that the Phoenician alphabet at Byblos had derived from the characters discovered at Ugarit, which were three centuries earlier. They argued; neither would yield an inch.

The fertile plain lay in the moonlight, and Jacques de Sirlan talked of the unexploited area which could so easily be irrigated.

"Why not by refugees?' I asked.

Angrily, Jacques explained that if the refugees showed any sign of settling in Syria they would forfeit all claim to Palestine.

"Why not leave the choice to them?' I persisted. 'Surely that would be better than stagnating with their children in the camps.'

"That would be playing straight into the hands of the Jews! Not that they would survive when the diaspora grew tired of shelling out millions of dollars.'

I let the argument drop uneasily. The deaf talk to the deaf, and political deadlock is the stale, familar ingredient in people's lives. Whether this red soil could sustain hundreds of thousands of refugees seemed the burning issue to the well-being, indeed the survival of so many, and what was its potential? Strangely, Syrian agriculture, once prosperous, has barely pulled through. A new class of landowners emerged after the Second World War. Mainly wealthy merchants they owned as many as sixty villages, each near Orontes, and ninety per cent of the Jezireh valley belonged to forty landlords. The results of intensive crop-farming were spectacular, but the soil lost its richness. In 1965 a hundredweight of fertilizer cost the same as nearly seven hundredweight of wheat, Syrian farmers used two lb. per acre compared with the hundred and thirty-two lb. used in France. Syria (like Iraq) did not produce any fertilizer. Nor did the owners reinvest their great profits. Socialism was on the way in, and they transferred their wealth to foreign banks, so that between 1954 and 1957 investments fell by half.

The Baath Party nationalized the larger farms in 1963. In 1968, the Baathists built an electric power station by the Orontes and, with help from the Italians, Czechs and Russians, set up the first nitrogenous fertilizer factory near the phosphate beds north of Palmyra. A second one is to be built at Homs. High-quality cotton was exchanged for Hungarian and Russian machinery. The most remarkable undertaking is the Takha dam across the Euphrates, eighty miles from Aleppo, built and financed with Russian aid to provide for a million and a half acres by 1974. The Khabour, tributary of the Euphrates, has been banked and canals have brought it under control providing two and a half million acres for farming. The country will soon have over five million acres of arable land and will no longer be at the mercy of floods and droughts. Iraq too, will feel the benefit. Even so, only a fifth of potential arable land is irrigated, and there is plenty of room for mechanized farming and for Palestinian refugees.

The Baron Hotel is Aleppo's cheerless answer to the Ritz. Frosted glass casts a mean light over drab corridors like a disused underground railway. But at least there was a bath and running water.

The light in the dining-room was dim, and the waiters padded among the grey table-cloths. My companion was an old man with a tender smile and an eye wrinkled with mischief and melancholy.

Piero Founi called across to him, asking about the Syrian Jews. How were they really treated? The old man's eyes glanced right and left like those of a startled bird as he tried to side-step Founi's hail of question. It was true they didn't go out at night, but only for their own protection . . . They could not leave the country, but could easily get permits to Damascus . . . The poor man muttered to me urgently that the Chief of Police was directly behind us. What he said was not really true; the Jews were having a terrible time; many were arrested; they were no longer permitted professions. It was dreadful, dreadful. Ssh!

I let my table-napkin fall and took stock of the local Beria. He resembled Francis Blanche's Gestapo chief in the film *Babette* – fat, puffed-up, complacent, revelling in his trade, watching humanity with small, piggish eyes, suspecting it of freedom.

Though Syria, unlike Iraq, has no official anti-Jewish legislation, the fifteen hundred Jews still in Syria are very much harassed and are regarded by the overbearing authorities as virtual Zionists. Every day someone is held in custody for forty-eight hours, although Assad's government is attempting some liberalisation.

Silvery Aleppo lay against a silver sky, with long, low, white houses and Moslem seminaries and mosques bristling with spiky minarets, animated by the swaying balance of shrouded women and the unhurried donkey-drivers urging their animals; timeless, hieratic, elegant.

The *souks* are the richest, most colourful markets in the country. Sheltered by stone arches hollowed out under the houses, they are grouped in guilds. There are blind beggars, peasants balancing basket-loads of chickens on their heads, black eyes glowing over veils, wealthy aggressive paunches and disdainful, striding Bedouins.

I wandered among the gold-embroidered table cloths, lengths of brocade and silver lamé, long white skins, smells of cinnamon and almond cakes baked golden. My friends were haggling in every corner. We had found our way to Ali Baba's cave, with all the splendour, glitter, clamour and sensuousness of the East.

From the chill we came into the pale rays of sun streaking the vast open space near the town centre. There was still the same serenity: donkey-drivers, two bicycles, and a dusty jeep by the fortress, looking like a toy.

The north wind turned cold, and I sheltered under the high vaults of the citadel on its rocky peak in the middle of the vast esplanade, ancient fortress and palace, and impressive token of the might that tastes of the Ommiad dynasty which dashed the hopes of the Frankish kings of Jerusalem.

The road ran dead straight to St Simeon, passing truncated cones of rock looking almost deliberate on the flinty desert. I never tire of these cruel ochre landscapes backed by the deep blue of the sky. We passed Bedouin women billowing with

91

coloured underskirts, with gold coins and gold chains round their necks, and black silk scarves tied hippy-style round their foreheads. A group of men, voluminous in brown wool coats with white turbans and cone-shaped crowns, and laden camels with red and black saddle cloths, broke their springy stride.

A broken pillar, 'its acanthus rubbed by winds of time, rough-handled by the passing centuries'* was Qalaat Semand, the home of St Simeon the Stylite. The romanesque basilica of white stone, encrusted with greys and golds, is one of the finest specimens of primitive Christian art, a sixth century tribute to Simeon's exemplary if somewhat acrobatic life. This ascetic hermit arrived in 412 with permission to live perched high on a column, which he extended metre by metre until it was thirty cubits high. He must have had a head for heights, for he spent twenty-seven years atop a variety of vertiginous pillars from which he bestowed his words on a ceaseless flow of pilgrims. He took, however, a great interest in everything: and on one occasion even spoke of St Geneviève the patroness of Paris, asking a Syrian merchant bound for France to convey his humble respects.

Goats and donkeys gazed on the magnificent, meagre, undulating hills of the region of the 'Dead Cities'. At one time northern Syria had many towns, but their inhabitants (mainly Nestorian Christians) drifted away in the sixth century to escape the Persian invasion. The exodus was complete by the time of the Arab conquest in the seventh century, and the cities which had been spared by armies fell to erosion and earthquakes.

Among the thorns, a complete façade was framed by trees and caught in the red afternoon sun, its colonnades, its pediments and its arched windows intact. Behind it lay ruins, but a fragmentary staircase led to a first floor which still had closets and armorial bearings. The life of a well-appointed household was strangely close, almost tangible. I could barely resist the impulse to walk on tiptoe.

Children emerged unexpectedly from the stone desert. An enchanting little girl with oyster-eyes and long fair hair trotted

* Guy Abéla in *Le Jour*, a Beyrouth French-speaking morning paper.

along beside me. She refused to be photographed until we gave her a coin. She took my hand and led me to her mother, a beautiful, fine-featured Bedouin woman with proud eyes and glorious 'crow's-wing' eyebrows. Heaped on her noble head with elegant dignity was a massive load of branches. She smiled, and removed her burden with a single, neat, assured movement and set it on my head. I tried to take it, but my bones turned to jelly and I felt uncomfortably concertinaed. She laughed, showing all her gold teeth. With a good deal of help I asked about her dentist in Aleppo and her bus-ride there and the fare of one pound (about twelve and a half pence).

She had five children, and was married at the same age as the girl with oyster-eyes, whose fair hair she stroked and who must have been about twelve. She had been married a long, long time, had never heard of Gamal Nasser, and had no radio and no electricity. I was sorry to leave her intelligent resourcefulness, and as we shook hands she was equally curious about me.

The hospitality of the Antaki family-home in Aleppo is the providence of travellers. The cool, vaulted cellars are lined with jars of jam and other goodies. We licked our lips shamelessly while the Antaki's son, Georges, opened any jar our eyes picked out. The old house was like a Mediterranean family-home with china, silverware, carpets, all good, quietly rich, easy to live with, old-fashioned.

There were merchants and industrialists talking sourly of the Baathist régime and its continual expropriations, censorship, and the absence of freedom of movement or speech. The bourgeoisie is a victim of the new régime; anticipating the future, many left after union with Egypt in 1958 and when the Baathists came to power in 1963. They were wise, for the government has well and truly steam-rollered the wealthy, cultured, French-speaking upper middle-class which chose to stay. They own no more now than a quarter of Syria's industry and live in the shadow of total nationalization.

The émigrés responded well to life in exile, and new industrial enterprises have grown up in the Lebanon, Europe, and even Africa. Clever, go-ahead, unrestricted by shortage of funds they have temperaments very far from the claustrophobic melancholy of their Syrian counterparts.

A charming young woman seemed particularly blighted. Damascus was terribly stifling; she could hardly breathe. Xenophobia was rampant; the authorities thought every second man a spy. Intellectual life had disappeared – plays, lectures and art exhibitions were things of the past. She did know someone in the censorship department, and browsed through French newspapers to 'blow a few cobwebs away', she said gloomily. It was especially poignant for her since Damascus was only forty miles from Beirut and she had many friends and relations in the Lebanon.

A striking young doctor with moderate views admired Israel's achievements and thought that, on ethnic and religious grounds, the Jews had as much right to live in Palestine as any Arab. As the wealthiest of Israel's neighbours, Syria should work with the Tel Aviv government to resettle the Palestinian refugees instead of allowing wounds to fester, or deliberately irritating it in order to create diversion. He told me about the scandalous black-market trade in U.N.R.W.A. products. In the Damascus flea market, U.N.R.W.A. blankets could be bought for about L12.00, and enormous sums paid by U.N.R.W.A. to Syrian aid organizations and certain Palestinian leaders disappeared without trace.

By dinner-time I had tired of the melancholy flavour of 'Old Russia' at the heart of this isolated, touchy, dwindling community.

Everyone spoke flawless French and imperfect English: they had been educated at convent schools and at the *lycée français*, all now closed by the government. Teaching today was in Arabic. French wasn't taught and English instruction was rudimentary. Much time was devoted to political indoctrination; with eighty children to a class clambering over desks and shouting their heads off, parents were taking turns to have small groups of children taught at home.

The menu was excellent and our hosts warm-hearted and attentive. They go to Europe on business every year and to take a cure. Their interests, though partly nationalized, are still considerable. The government has preserved established structures when toppling them might create a vacuum always risky in the world of finance.

At midnight, with coffee still unserved, we sleepily abandoned this marooned, decimated society to its ineluctable and melancholy fate.

A green plain stretched endlessly away, with acres of wheat and red soil: the scenery south towards Damascus was like Normandy without the apples. Rolling grasslands, with flocks of sheep and goats, and camels looking forlorn in the thinning vegetation; vast rocky steppes, where Bedouins' tents, open at the front, were set like scarabs. Today 'Bedouin' is the name of any nomadic tribesman in this part of the world, but in the last century it meant a camel-breeding nomad superior to mere goat and sheep-breeders.

The desert opened up brown and vast and seemed immeasurable, though bounded by a soft distant line of mountains.

Hama was one of the few towns to hold out against the crusaders: its narrow streets were full of shadows. Enormous upright wheels of dark wood drew water from the Orontes for the town and the fields around. The black and white minarets are a little like Florentine churches. We stopped to see a cool, delightful little seventeenth-century palace with fine wood panelling, embellished with landscapes and murmuring fountains in marble courtyards.

East towards Palmyra, the desert blinded us. The talk became extreme. 'The Palestinians . . . the Jews . . . Hussein . . . Al Fatah' the same old tags buzzing like flies.

A fat man on a bicycle stopped at our stand-up picnic by the road beside a foul-smelling pond. In broken French he told me of the scandalous Madame d'Andurain who, in the thirties, long before Saint-Tropez conferred sanction on the custom, used to sunbathe here in the nude. He seemed quite worked up about it.

Palmyra was a light, timeless enchantment. Many of the sculptures on the city tombs are touching, though one, depicting a whole family on its pediment, was comically supported by the pipeline of the Iraq Petroleum Company. Another pipe takes Syrian oil from Karatchok, a hundred miles south, to Tartous, where a third pipe, a joint Iraqi-Syrian enterprise, brings oil from North Rumeilah in Iraq.

Desert images slipped by a flaming golden sunset, the occasional sculpture or broken architrave. The Hôtel de la Reine Zénobie is old-fashioned, vast as a barn, with small, sputtering stoves warming the tiled floors of the big whitewashed rooms. In the bar, sitting on low, carpet-covered seats, sipping cold champagne, everyone helped piece together the city. It was a difficult task, for, like most towns in the area it is extremely ancient, dating from the Akkadian era, two thousand years before Christ. It became a great city under the Romans, and especially under Hadrian, who rebuilt Jerusalem. It was a major port of call for caravans conveying merchandise from Persia, India and China to the Mediterranean harbours. In the third century A.D., Queen Zenobie ruled there. This remarkable woman successfully waged war on Rome, and, not content with her independence, she set out to conquer Egypt and Asia Minor, but she was taken as a prisoner to Rome where Emperor Aurelian spared his turbulent captive.

Today's visitors to Palmyra will also hear about the exploits of another woman, equally eager for conquests though they were somewhat smaller in scope. Marga d'Andurain founded the Hôtel de la Reine Zénobie in the twenties, when the country was under French mandate. The hotel was a regular haunt for desert-corps officers. Mme d'Andurain was apparently a good deal more than friendly with them. Eyes pop out of their heads as the older locals confirm how she used to sunbathe in the nude. There had been a Monsieur d'Andurain, a retired army officer endowed, one imagines, with uncommon tolerance. She either killed him or arranged his killing by a Berber to whom the unfortunate man

*Above* 'Salam alekum' to the guard, standing on top of the *ziggurat* overlooking the vast, dusty plain

*Right* Guards watching over the huge, truncated pyramid of greyish bricks, the great *ziggurat* of Ur

In the marshland, the smiling fishermen greeted us; nearby are their long black, slim boats, tapered like gondolas, caulked with bitumen

The houses, *mudhifs*, are domo-roofed and built of layered reeds and mud

*Above* Against the ruins of one of the 'dead Cities', a Bedouin woman and her five children

*Right* Across the Syrian plain, the desert opens up brown and vast. A part of the old Roman road to Palmyra

*Below* The Palace Azem, ancient residence of a governor of Damascus

A street of old Bosra, a market-town of three thousand inhabitants, in the middle of the Druze country

With the Roman walls of Bosra in the background, Druze women with velvet robes and violet eyes

had lent a large sum. 'Lend money to a friend and lose the money and the friend.'\* Poor M. d'Andurain! She bribed another Berber from the hotel's stables into a marriage of convenience, as she had long wanted to visit Mecca (forbidden to Christians). Her strategy succeeded when the helpful Berber guided her through a pilgrimage, dressed as a man. But he incurred her wrath by attempting to assert his marital rights. However unexpected and surprising this new-found virtue (unless he was as ugly as sin), she doctored his food or drink and became a widow again. Legends inspire wilder legends: that she worked for the Deuxième Bureau or British Intelligence or both, or was a Soviet double-agent. After the Second World War the unfortunate lady met the fate she had been handing out so generously, at the hands of a German legionnaire, who threw her overboard somewhere off Tangiers after some sombre traffic in smuggled cigarettes.

An old Syrian gentleman spoke to me of her with real affection. 'She was remarkably slim, you know, and the sun had turned her skin gold. I last saw her by a roadside. She had been raped by three Bedouins who had ambushed her car, but she seemed to take it all quite calmly.'

Palmyra village is a few low-roofed houses strung along the road. Thin, bitter-sweet music came from a dim-lit café. The dark was pierced by a hurricane lamp held by a tall Bedouin draped in white, riding side-saddle on a biblical spotless she-ass. The lamp was West German and according to the white apparition 'never went out'. He asked after General de Gaulle – *le Raïs de la France*. 'The French were here in the old days,' he said; 'they weren't such bad times.' Even apparitions angle for baksheesh. He disappeared back into the dark, jogging on his she-ass.

The country became hilly, stony and less cultivated. An icy wind sent clouds across the Buqaia plain. The Krack des Chevaliers dominates the plain, dank, sinister, indestructible and overpowering, sited where the giant fortress of Hisn-al-Akrad housed his

\* Sephardic proverb.

Kurdish guards on the Damascus route. Raymond of Tripoli besieged it unsuccessfully, and was nearly imprisoned there while his own citadel and lands were under attack from the mighty Saladin, so that war-worn Raymond turned the problems of the Krack over to the Hospitallers (who fared no better).

In the great courtyard with its tall foiled arches we said good-bye to our friends. They were heading for Beirut while Leila, Founi and I continued on to Damascus.

The New Ommeyade Hotel was luxury after the Hotel Baron. Our arrival stirred a group of healthy young Russian pilots, spread about on brown plush cushions under the fronded shade of a tall green plant.

A hot bath, by courtesy of the Baathists, was followed by another dinner, this time with a restless, impish little man, born well-to-do under the old régime and apparently now a skilled broker for the new one. His drawing-room had Damascene furniture of precious woods inlaid with mother-of-pearl. The room was upholstered in fine carpet from Bukhara, silky to the touch. The rest of the house, as so often in the east, would be full of Louis XV fakes and doubly-gilded opalines.

Israel was under attack, of course, but it was fairly restrained; against Lebanon and the Lebanese it was a good deal more vehement: they were traders in the temple who only think of money. A deceitful press was misinforming the French about the Arab situation. Pindar called silence the highest form of human wisdom, and no Arab country has more vociferous foes than its Arab neighbours.

The French cultural attaché insisted that French influence was still considerable, that the language was still taught in schools, despite the inflexible tactlessness of the Church, which had resulted in the monks and nuns being locked away in their convents and monasteries, powerless to influence events or opinions. The French government gave eighty scholarships a year to the highly-gifted Syrian students who would one day form the meritocracy. A university teacher launched a violent attack on the inadequacy of courses and the ignorance of students, making the

Syrian intellectuals sound like half-wits. As he was an official, I decided he was being slightly provocative.

Damascus has the blare, bustle, crowded pavements, heavy traffic of a real city, fast-moving, clamorous, but with a calm almost haughty immutability. The light is like golden dust and the architecture white and rounded, softened by bougainvilleas and fountains. The Palace Azem (pronounced 'Azm'), ancient residence of governor of Damascus, was a perfect example.

There were the inevitable *souks* and stalls and milling throngs, and the haggling and garrulous, gesticulating, ever-protesting traders. With sharp cries, peasants from the Hauran cleared a way for their laden donkeys. A rare tourist, though dazed by the rich sounds and colours may trace a brilliant shaft of sun back through the square aperture on the high, overhead vaulting. The stalls were stocked not only with Syrian jewellery and bric-à-brac but with imported shoes, woollens, household utensils and cleaning materials. General Assad's government allowed various consumer goods from abroad, presumably to cheer the place up after the severity of the previous régime.

When I last visited the museum, there were only bare plinths and fly-blown windows, and everything had been hidden away in the cellars for fear of Israeli air-raids. The Doura Europos Synagogue was also barred and bolted, apparently to prevent people from visiting the shrine of an accursed faith, even a seventeen-hundred-years-old one. Now there were still troops everywhere, armoured cars at each road junction, and sentries clutching machine-guns outside government buildings; but the Hellenistic bronzes, the statues from Ras Shamra, and the pottery from Raqqa were up from the cellars. Even the Jewish faith was slightly less accursed, and the faded frescoes of the Doura Europos Synagogue were being shown to a party of school-children. Baathism was at last becoming more liberal. The museum gardens smelt of eucaylptus. A young guide, inquiring if I spoke English, proceeded to explain everything in Arabic. Outside I was waylaid by a braided, uniformed attendant who pointed

dramatically at each statue, exclaiming 'Monsieur!' or 'Madame!' lest I be unable to tell one from the other. An unarmed Fedayeen in camouflage uniform asked for money, and when I slipped him a few coins he stared at them, totted them up and then returned them, looking extremely dissatisfied.

Across the thoroughfare lies Suleiman's mosque, an example of islamic architecture, rising softly from among ancient yews. Fighter-planes were dotted among the trees but I ignored them apart from making sure that they did not get into my photographs.

A neat European-dressed middle-aged man bore down on me, asking if I spoke English and then how interested I was in military matters. Only then did I see a sign saying 'Military Museum'. I decided to act simple, expressing great enthusiasm for this really remarkable specimen of sixteenth-century architecture. The poor man was too far out of his depth, but nevertheless ushered me into a room rather ominously designated 'French Atrocities during the Mandate'. The exhibits were chiefly from the campaign of General Gouraud, who entered Damascus on 25 July 1920 and ousted King Feisal whom Colonel Lawrence had hurriedly set on the throne to steal a march on the French who, Lawrence thought, had no rights in the Middle East. Photographs of heaps of bodies, men suspended from gallows, angry slogans, all denounced the French and the Americans. I examined them thoughtfully and in silence before turning to my 'guide'. I inquired where he had learned his English. Apparently it was in Washington, and, though he claimed to be retired, every uniformed policeman who passed saluted him.

I bade him a brisk goodbye as if suddenly remembering an appointment, and strode away; but he ran after me and caught my arm demanding my name. I repeated it four times and he wrote it down in his notebook.

My archaeological antennae were at work on André Parrot, lunching with the French ambassador, François Charles-Roux and his wife, all of whom know every inch of every road in Syria and were a mine of valuable information.

The Residence, built in the Turkish occupation, was half-buried in bougainvilleas, and we chatted under a sweet-smelling vine arbour. Since 1933, apart from the interruption of war, Parrot had been in charge of excavations on the middle part of the Euphrates. He discovered Mari, the city of the Amorites, a Semitic people from the west who drove out the Akkadian kings in the nineteenth century B.C.

The discovery of Mari had exploded like a bombshell in Middle Eastern archaeology. A group of peasants burying one of their kinsmen came upon a statue and brought it to Parrot who had started work in the area, believing that Mari lay there. Beside himself with joy, he dispatched the priceless windfall to the Louvre, and one can imagine his impatience as he waited for the reply. Meanwhile he cabled Paris to announce the discovery of eight more statues, one bearing the inscription 'Mari, king of Mari'. It was an incomparable moment. His theories had been proved right: Mari was underfoot and all around him. While news of his triumph journeyed over the wires, he found four more statues, again confirming the discovery. The long-awaited answer from the Louvre arrived, cursorily dismissing the statue as a 'crude figure'. Obviously it wasn't the Mona Lisa, but the scientific and archaeological importance of the find was entirely wasted on the arbiters at the Louvre!

The traffic slowed; vehicles were being filtered one by one among a good many armoured cars with Bren-guns directed to the sky. We worked our way on to the southbound road to the Hauran and Druze country, Druzia, as Guy Abéla calls it. The same ochre backgrounds were turning gold in the rising sun. Willows rustled, and occasionally we passed through thin, sprawling villages of mud-brick houses, with a few stalls, donkeys, and a bicycle or two, and bright peasant women with gold coins in their ears. Then came the great plain again, rich, red, green, cultivated, sprouting corn. A tractor. A peasant isolated in a field. Black basaltic rocks appeared, and the villages were gloomy with the black stone and dark mud-bricks. The smell of Syria was everywhere, the tang of cinnamon-scented dust. Red flowers on the wild fruit-trees, and lines of tarpaulin-covered lorries from Kuwait and Jordan fitted with both Jordanian and Israeli plates, the latter covered with a soiled rag, were bringing phosphates from the Jordanian port of Aqaba, or vegetables from west-bank Jordan and even Israel, where they passed without hindrance of any kind.

The citadel of Bosra almost encircles the ruins of the Roman theatre. The curator, a heavily-built man of about fifty with a warm, generous smile and a perfect command of French, who had studied with Dunant in southern Italy, told us of the Arabs who had invaded the city in the seventh century and at first bivouacked in the theatre, blocking the vomitories and building a defensive wall round the theatre, later adding a series of towers. Thus the citadel helped to preserve the Roman theatre through the ages, and its black stones give a mournful beauty. It resembles fortresses erected by the crusaders four centuries later, when the Christians employed Arab labour whose skills were handed down.

Modern Bosra is an agricultural market-town of three thousand inhabitants, standing in the middle of a dark, fertile plain. The streets are made of hardened mud, and the low, flat-roofed houses of black stone. Children clustered around, and here, in the heart of Druze country, both men and women were in black, with baggy trousers gathered in at the ankle: the women in long veils, the men in turbans. They were tall and stately, with remarkably handsome features, and often with bright blue eyes.

A wedding party was signalled from afar by the loud jingle of tambourines as we rounded a bend in one of the narrow streets. The men wore brilliant reds and blues, and though they put their hands in front of my camera there was no hostility and they did it smilingly.

Working round some Roman ruins I came upon a diamond-shaped carving on a wall. The diamond was subdivided into squares, and was the original plan of the city of Tyre, which had later been adopted as the town's emblem. Among a few walls and still-standing capitals the same emblem was chalked on the ground by a bunch of children playing hopscotch.

An old man with china-blue eyes and a shock of white hair surmounted by a black skullcap invited us into the house which he and his wife shared with his son and daughter-in-law. A large room had a big double bed with white sheets, and the walls and concrete floor were covered with carpets.

Our curator showed us the ruins of Shabbah and the Philippeion, the theatre of Philip, where he had just cleared the floor of a Byzantine basilica, and he told us of mosaics which he had uncovered and protected with layers of earth. The *Guide Bleu* described these achievements to Dunant and the Museum of Damascus; but the curator is a nice man.

Three hundred black goats jostled up the street, passing a pylon of four tall pillars along the main avenue, where flies buzzed round busy stalls laden with fruit or almond-filled pastries. The old herdswoman, a Shakespearean witch or Death itself, lifted a scraggy arm and nodded her toothless head at my *'Marhaba'*. There were more camels and turbans, and women in full velvet dresses with long white veils framing their faces, and rows of gold coins around their necks.

Our next stop was Shakka, where we walked far too long among the huts, stinking of dried dung, and the Roman walls. The Druze people were superb. They were descendants of the Iranian Zoroastrians who swept north from the domination of the Acheminid Persians in the sixth century. Everywhere were women with violet eyes. In Kanawat, by a Byzantine monastery, a magnificent young man with a thin moustache, and his father, a noble white turbaned figure from a Persian print, invited me to share their meal (which was a good deal less alluring than they).

The Druze country is proud and austere, beautiful and restrained like its noble inhabitants. I understand the love felt for Syria by some of the French troops and officials during the Mandate. The country grows on one.

After the lorry-loads of the army camp, Damascus shows not

the slightest sign of war, and the evening throngs spilled on to the pavement, calm and cheerful as could be.

We dined in the Ali-Baba; over-ornate, marbled, gilded, multicoloured, but with exquisite local food. An official party sat beside us: one Syrian, one Asiatic, one Syrian, one Asiatic; there were twenty-five of them. They were North Koreans, whispered the head waiter, and their conversation didn't look exactly effortless: perhaps they discussed the weather, or the cooking, or maybe Chairman Mao (who rated very high in Syria). General Hafez-el-Assad criticized Syria's over-dependence on the Soviet Union. In 1969, when Atassi was seeking arms from Moscow and, not surprisingly, did not get them, the Chinese, quick to take advantage of an opportunity, promised missiles to the Syrians and did send their celebrated machine-guns to be used by guerrillas in action. Everyone promised everything to everyone.

Our host that evening hailed the present Syrian régime. After Baathist – Socialist austerity, General Assad was popular and authority was beginning to be human. Inspired by Nasser's example, Assad was building a political structure close to that of Egypt, with a President heading the executive, appointed by the party, ratified by the People's Council, and approved by popular majority.

Our host cared little for politics except when they touched his way of life, and he was well-attuned to the haggling, the backscratching and the use of influence essential in the East, whoever is in power. The present government had halted nationalization, and there was still room for a sharp, resourceful little man like our host. Alas, his friends in high places might topple at every coup, and he neeeded them, which made life expensive. A dozen hand-made ties for one; a week with a girl in Beirut for another. In Moscow you sold Syrian cotton and picked up second-grade machinery. You nipped over to Budapest, where the Hungarians bought mere cotton to sell to the West for hard currencies. They never looked at the stuff and slipped ten per cent of the deal to our friendly lizard or chameleon. He'd seen the inside of several prisons, but someone invariably gets you out after a day or so. It sounded like a real Comrades' Republic. He was appalled that I had admitted coming to Damascus to interview people, and briefed me that he would tell the police, when they questioned him, that I was the daughter of a friend of his father and just 'passing through'.

The only Englishman in Syria (a rather handsome man with brown hair and blue eyes, the local agent of the Iraq Petroleum Company) joined us. Apparently he spent most of his time in his club in Damascus; he seemed remarkably vague about oil.

The hotel valet seemed crestfallen at my departure. I gave him a tip to allay his sorrow and he gave me three flowers wrapped in Kleenex. He had always been extremely cordial, with an odd habit of investing every action with an aura of mystery, so that he would sidle up to me, with the wariness of an arch-conspirator, to present a cake of soap. Once I asked for two pairs of shoes I had entrusted to him that morning. There was a stealthy tap at the door and he brought one shoe only, retaining the others, presumably, as a pretext for a farewell visit.

Across the familiar landscape again and at the Lebanese frontier a group of unarmed Fedayeen* wearing their panther-like uniforms and Biegeard caps, were pumping up the spare tyre of a lorry, with another larger group killing time in the sun.

A great press of people waited at the border to get out of the country. My taxi-driver casually overtook the queue, drew up in front of a Druze sheikh crossing from the Lebanon, completed the formalities in a trice, and we were on our way.

While this was going on, three armed Syrian soldiers dragged the driver from a Saudi Arabian lorry, beat him about until there

* The Syrian army has calmly absorbed the four thousand members of the Saika, the foremost guerrilla organization, regarding this as the most effective way of keeping them under control. Moreover, Syria had closed her frontier with Jordan, thereby slamming the door in the faces of the Jordanian guerrillas. It is safe to assume, therefore, that the country is not drained of guerrillas.

was blood on the man's white *arabaya* and dragged him into a hut. 'Damned fool,' my driver muttered. 'He jumped the queue.'

In Syria, our driver had driven at twenty, the embodiment of wariness and restraint. In the Lebanon he was a different man, overtaking on the inside, on bends, and on the brows of hills, ignoring lines of any colour, and rarely doing less than ninety.

After that hair-raising journey, I was relieved to reach the Phénicia. I ran a bath and read a letter from my daughter telling me how cold and grey it was in Paris. I had just enough energy for the hairdresser. And then I went straight to sleep.

# Israel

AN Iraqi visa is suspect here, and the immigration officer in his navy-blue uniform stared peevishly from the depths of his narrow cubicle. He was shoulder to shoulder with an attractive, dark-haired girl to whom he was showing the ropes. He interrupted his tuition and thumbed through the list of *personae non gratae*.

The Arab visas on my French passport perplexed him deeply. He turned the pages, muttering to the pretty girl, and glanced again at the black list before coming back to my troublesome document. The line of tourists behind me grew longer and longer. They were sweating and heavily draped with cameras and small blue Pan-Am grips. It was the start of the Easter holidays. My legs ached and my patience was wearing thin. I cast my eyes imploringly to heaven. The gesture was only half complete, when fortunately they lighted on the General Haim Herzog, the Israeli radio commentator and former chief of the Israeli Intelligence. He dispatched an angel of mercy, and after a brief whispered word to the immigration officer (who thought by now that I was some Shin-bet Mata-Hari) the general had his arms warmly around me and my passport, doubly agreeable, for General Herzog, the son of a former Chief Rabbi of Dublin, looks like a handsome Irish guardsman.

His wife Aura hovered nearby, small, clever, sensitive as a golden quail. Born in Cairo, she was educated, like everyone, in an Ursuline convent. She had told me the year before about her son cooped up in a blockhouse near the Canal, under Egyptian fire. Her voice had faltered, and she had lapsed into a silence of incommunicable feelings drawn from pride and courage and fear.

The night was mild, starry and mellow, and the road cut through strong-scented orange groves. Leaving Tel Aviv, I lost all sense of direction among the multitude of cars and thoroughfares, no-entry signs, red lights, 'turn right', 'turn left', 'straight ahead'. A Yemenite driver directed me in gruff Hebrew. 'Shmolla, shmolla', he shouted, tucking an extra 'h' into the word, but jabbing his finger to the left so that I found my way into the noisy darkness of Petah Tikvah. The town was a large one, founded at the end of the nineteenth century by the Russian and Polish Jews of the second aliyah. Members of this second wave of immigration considered themselves superior to the first, who had started flowing into Palestine fifty years before. In America, Australia and elsewhere the earliest immigrants and their descendants ruled the roost, becoming local aristocracy. Here what mattered was an immigrant's motive, not the time of his arrival.

The first aliyah in 1881 was of refugees from the pogroms in Poland and Russia. Some settled in Jerusalem, where three-quarters of the forty-thousand population was Jewish, but most went to farming colonies and worked on the land bought from Arab peasants by Baron Edmond de Rothschild or Sir Moses Montefiore. The third aliyah, precipitated by Nazism in the thirties, was also of political refugees. It was the second aliyah of idealists and intellectuals which provided Palestine with its Jewish upper crust. High-minded, uncompromising Zionists, disciples of Herzl, they were true pioneers ready to combat malaria, dysentery, drought and a hostile population. They were the driving force which established the independent state and made up the first official government of Israel. The intelligentsia of this nascent society, guardians of the True Law, they scraped the flinty soil of Judea and drained pestilence-ridden Galilee to found sweet-smelling orchards and thriving kibbutzim.

'Yerushalaim,' I shouted, hopefully trying for the right pronunciation, and a motorist in a tee-shirt directed me with a well-intentioned flow of Hebrew. I thought I detected 'Ya-mi-na' which, if it meant the same as it did in Arabic, meant I should turn right. I did so and found a hut built on a terrace, calling itself 'café-restaurant'.

I sat at a laminated table with a small cup of steaming, scented mocha from a large lady with a green blouse, who gurgled and waved her arms and somehow told me she was an Iraqi.

'Baghdad?' I inquired.

*'Ken.'* ('Yes.')

*'Tov.'* ('Beautiful!')

*'Ken-Tov,'* she agreed ecstatically.

'Petah Tikvsh?'

Contemptuous gurglings, this time, but 'Tel Aviv *tov,'* she conceded.

The first Turkish coffee is like Proust's *madeleine.* Its bitter-mellow taste has all the delights of the East. I like it *masbut,* slightly sweetened, and sniff it first, take a sip, then begin to gulp it gently even if it is hot enough to burn my mouth. The first coffee immediately links me with a world I love in an almost secret way.

The orange groves sparkle with golden fruit, and their heavy, crisp smell floats with you all the way to the Bab-el-Wad pass. The pass leads up through rocks and pine-forests to Jerusalem. Until recently, it was still lined with the burnt-out hulks of the convoy of Jewish lorries ambushed by Arabs in 1948, with a few sheaves of flowers preserving the memory of the men who died there.

The British made Palestine a 'twice-promised land'. Obsessed with the protection of the trade-route to India, they watched uneasily the southward spread of the Russian Empire. For fifty years after the opening of the Suez Canal, Britain's strategists argued that her surest defence of the Empire lay in the twenty thousand square miles of Sinai sand on the east bank of the

Canal. Then one night in February 1915 a Turkish column appeared suddenly and crossed the Canal in a lighter hauled across the desert. They were cut to pieces by the Royal Navy, but their raid altered strategic thinking and Kitchener, the British Resident in Cairo, fearing that next time the landing-force might be a powerful French or Russian army, decided on a new line of defence further from the Canal. Thus Palestine was to become, in Lloyd George's phrase, 'le Tampon protecteur de l'Egypte', and the Royal Navy acquired the first-class port of Haifa, to which the British ran a railway from the oil-fields which had become a Mesopotamian goldmine.

In July 1915, when the Sultan's armies were humiliating the British troops, Britain embarked on an audacious adventure with Colonel Lawrence who was to whip up nationalism among the Arabs and provoke them to destroy the Turkish empire from within. This bold enterprise was conceived months before the outbreak of the Second World War, when a shy young Arab prince arrived in Cairo and called on Kitchener. He was the second son of Sherif Hussein, whose absolute religious Moslem authority descended from the Prophet. Hussein was governor of Mecca and Medina, the holiest places of Islam, and he had sent his son to discover Britain's intentions if the Arabs rose against the Turks, which they might do when Hussein himself gave the signal.

This unexpected new political entity, uniting all the Arabs under Britain's wing and stretching from the Persian Gulf to Turkey was to mature in London. It took eighteen months and eight letters for Sir Henry MacMahon, Kitchener's successor in Cairo to conclude an agreement that the Arabs would rise against Ottoman rule, and in return Britain would establish an independent Arab kingdom when the war was over. The boundaries of the kingdom were unspecified and Palestine was never mentioned. Years later, on 17 April 1939, MacMahon told *The Times* that he had had no intention of 'including Palestine in the zone of Arab independence'. Yet in the minutes of a War Cabinet's Eastern Committee's meeting on 27 November 1918, the Prime Minister, Lord Curzon, declared, 'The promise made to Hussein in 1915 included Palestine among the regions which were in future to be independent.' The Arabs thus imagined that Palestine would soon be theirs, while Britain was planning an international mandate, a British protectorate, and the creation of a Jewish National Home for Zionists. Lawrence approved, since it would keep the French out. He loathed 'those people' who were demanding a place in which Britain had established a divine authority.

The French pressed doggedly for their rights as co-victors, and Britain listened, as she listened also to Russia, who demanded a foot in the Holy Land to safeguard the welfare of the Orthodox community.

Of the two men who were sent to sort out an agreement, Mark Sykes was an orientalist, and Charles François Georges-Picot an experienced French diplomat. By March 1916 these two sincere idealists had decided that Arab Asia, but not the Arabian peninsula, should be divided into two spheres of influence. As such a decision would much reduce the significance of Britain's promises to Sherif Hussein, the Anglo-French agreement was kept secret, and even Sir Henry MacMahon, who was still British High Commisssioner in Egypt, did not know of it until Sykes told him during a visit to Cairo.

The following year the terms were revealed in a Bolshevik publication and caused violent indignation among the Arabs. Over-riding France and Russia, Britain had Suez placed under international control as a first step towards her future mandate. She had two trump cards. One was an army of three hundred thousand men in Egypt. In September 1917, in order to safeguard the Suez Canal and pave the way for Palestine, Lloyd George chose a little-known cavalry general from the Somme front, Edmund Henry Allenby, to drive an offensive north. He had one order: Jerusalem must be captured before Christmas.

The second trump was a two thousand-year-old dream. In a letter of 2 November 1917 to Sir Walter Rothschild, Sir Arthur Balfour approved something which not Titus nor Godfrey of

Bouillon nor Saladin nor Tamerlane nor any caliph of Islam had ever even envisaged: the return of the exiled Jews.

Hussein and Faisal swallowed the so-called 'Balfour Declaration' and Hussein was even persuaded that he could win the grateful support of international Jewry for the cause of Arab independence, and that the Jewish immigration would not entail the slightest 'political and economic disadvantage' for the local people. His acquiescence was obtained but nothing was ever written down.

In 1918 Chaim Weizmann was a distinguished Zionist chemist living in Britain who had devised a process for the industrial manufacture of acetone, essential to the composition of explosives used for the war effort. He had the gratitude of several cabinet members including Lloyd George and Churchill, and Lawrence, who admired Weizmann, introduced the chemist to his own protégé Faisal (second son of Hussein), whom Lawrence had chosen above the shy Abdullah whom he thought too intelligent. Faisal and Weizmann were both bitter about the Sykes-Picot agreement, and Weizmann assured Faisal that the Jews would help him to build a strong and prosperous kingdom within the framework of a British protectorate in Palestine. They would be good neighbours and no threat to the Arabs, for the Jews would never be a great power and would only serve to guarantee the country's economic development, so that the four or five million new immigrants could be absorbed without threat to the rights of the Arab peasants, since 'there was no lack of arable lands in that part of the world'.

The return of the Jews concerned Britain less in terms of Jewish destiny than in those of her own political ambitions. She would acquire an ally and 'major new responsibilities' to argue for the right to administer Palestine alone. Only a formal mandate would turn the country into a proper buffer between 'her' canal and the French in Syria and the Lebanon. Sir Arthur Balfour's letter, however, had one restricting clause: 'Nothing should be done which might prejudice the civil and religious rights of the non-Jewish communities.' This was a generous

112

statement of intent, but rather vague, as Sir Arthur did not say how this could be brought about. So the poison was planted by the absence of any practical application for implementing the Balfour Declaration. The benefits of this opportunism ran out at first light on a drab May morning thirty years later, when the Union Jack was lowered and General Cunningham, Commander of the British Forces, departed from Jerusalem without a farewell to the Arab authorities or the leaders of the Jewish community.

Already on Easter Sunday 1920 six Arabs and six Jews had died in a savage riot which erupted outside the Jaffa Gate and renewed the bloodshed that is the country's history.

Britain, entrusted with the responsibility of Palestine by the 1922 League of Nations Mandate, tried to stem this violence by her military presence, and, torn between her conflicting obligations, found herself unable to control the events she had unleashed.

Jews had flocked to Palestine, and between 1922 and 1937 three hundred thousand immigrants quadrupled the Jewish population, while the country grew by only 150,000 acres. Fifteen thousand refugees from Nazi persecution arrived in 1936. To afford the Jews some degree of protection from the numerous Arab population, the British authorities stamped out insurrection, killing more than twelve hundred Arabs. The problem became more acute with each new boatload of Jews, and the British government set up a series of commissions of inquiry to seek a path to peace. They all foundered on the same problem: how to give the Jews a home without impairing the rights of the Arab population.

Whitehall arranged a conference in London on 7 February 1939, at which Jews and Arabs would sit around the same table and thrash out their problems. It was finally convened, but each side adopted such irreconcilable positions that no real exchange took place.

As another world war loomed, Britain's policy changed and she decided to appease the Arab world. In a White Paper of 17 May 1939, the government effectively rescinded Balfour's promise by imposing a limit of seventy-five thousand on the number of Jews who would be allowed to settle in Palestine over the next five years, and placing severe restrictions on Jewish land-purchases.

Sixteen years later Clement Attlee broadcast his determination to pursue the policy of the White Paper of 1939. This announcement, on the holiday of Yom Kippur, the Day of Atonement, stunned Jews everywhere. In Palestine it seemed the British Labour party was behaving incomprehensibly for, through international socialist movements, the Zionists had secured a promise that when the Labour Party came to power there was to be concerted immigration to establish a Jewish majority in Palestine and to encourage the Arabs to 'move out as the Jews moved in'.

Attlee's foreign policy was to be carried out by a product of the British trade-union movement. Ernest Bevin arrived at the Foreign Office with little knowledge of world affairs but unshakeable confidence in man's commonsense. He made Palestine the focal point of his attention. He soon saw the complexity of the problem he had chosen to solve and, advised by Arabists who held sway in the Foreign Office, among them Sir Harold Beeley, he began to discover that the Arabs had legitimate rights in Palestine.

The waves of violence unleashed by the Arab community three years before subsided while the rest of the world went to war. Opposition to any resumption of Jewish immigration was inflexible. Ernest Bevin was warned that any modification of the policies of the White Paper would have a most injurious effect on Anglo-Arab relations, and Britain's supply of oil would be imperilled. His attitude was shaped less by such fears than by personal conviction. Had Britain any right to reduce the Arab community in Palestine to a minority after seven hundred years? Bevin failed to realize that the Zionists had changed and that, in the post-war world, Jews numbed by genocide were determined to establish a home for those who somehow survived the nightmare. They would no longer argue the merits of their claims; they sought action and would fight. In August 1945 the

Labour government received their demands: a hundred thousand immigration permits, and an immediate official declaration that Palestine would be a Jewish State.

As time ran out, any compromise seemed impossible. Any solution would arouse extremists and would have to be imposed by force. Yet Bevin believed in common sense and patient negotiation, even for Palestine. With refreshing ingenuousness, he tried to reconcile the claims of Arabs and Jews as he would have tackled an industrial dispute in a Coventry smelting-works. Though he called the sides together around a conference table, he had decided to allay further Arab intransigence by maintaining the restrictive policies of the White Paper.

After centuries of shrewdness and despite a degree of Machiavellism in its diplomacy, this was a naïve decision for Britain to make, and it brought the British people two years of bloodshed. Fatefully, the decision to stand by the White Paper was announced on the day when the Jews, united in prayer, were counting the cost of the holocaust and extolling a return to the Promised Land. The Jewish Agency resorted to terrorism, and saboteurs of Irgun and the Stern Gang struck in support of the Haganah's underground army.

Ill-prepared for a police role, the British army reacted brutally, losing many of its own troops. Like every other army, it used mass repression which stirred up further violence, tightening the bonds between the Jewish population and the extremists. Their immediate demand was for a hundred thousand immigration permits for the Jews still rotting in the displaced persons' camps, and the Zionists resolved to get by force what the British refused to give them by law.

Through a secret network of extraordinarily effective and imaginative organizers, they delivered thousands of Jews to the Mediterranean ports and set them aboard a motley, derelict armada of battered Canadian corvettes, ancient shrimp-boats from Louisiana, excursion steamers, river barges, anything with a propeller that would float to Palestine. Landings were usually on moonless nights on deserted beaches between Tel Aviv and Haifa, where the passengers jumped into the water to reach the Promised Land. Often the vessels were intercepted by British warships and taken back to Cyprus and new camps for the desperate human cargo.

Photographs of emaciated victims of Nazi persecution, forcibly taken from overcrowded hulks and sent back to captivity, appeared in every newspaper in the free world, arousing world sympathy for the Zionist cause. The Arabs, by refusing to discuss the fate of these victims, created an antipathy that buried the real question which was, why had the Great Powers themselves failed to offer homes to the refugees?

The United States Congress refused to vote in President Truman's bill and revive the country's tradition of generous hospitality. During ten months of 1945 and 1946, the richest nation in the world, arguing that an Arab population of 1,250,000 should welcome the influx of a quarter of a million Jews, herself took in 4,765 refugees – a number smaller than the human cargo of the Exodus. Britain took none at all, but beaten, plundered, humiliated France, always a haven for the afflicted, behaved more charitably. She sheltered and fed the refugees from her feeble resources, and protected those engaged in shepherding them abroad. Her army, police, politicians and port authorities turned a blind eye or gave tangible help to the networks organizing illicit immigration. False documents were made available, as well as transport, ships, planes, airfields, even guns for their protection. Long after the embargo was lifted, General Dayan told me, 'France has harmed us, but no harm can equal the good she once did us, which we shall never forget.'

England and America were unstinting only in the number of their investigators and researchers who journeyed through Palestine. In the end they advised against a Jewish state but recommended an increase in immigration. The Jews were furious, so were the Arabs. The two were in agreement for once.

Sabotage followed with a vengeance and neither the Haganah, nucleus of the future army, nor the Irgun and Stern Gang gave any quarter. They mined roads and railway bridges, locomotive works and every possible target. They kidnapped six of His Britannic Majesty's officers.

Things were becoming too much for the British army and on 'Black Saturday', 29 June 1945, the paratroops carried out a massive round-up of two thousand, seven hundred Jews, including four leading members of the Jewish Agency, and a warrant was issued for the arrest of David Ben Gurion. In three weeks the terror reached a new level, when an Irgun commando-group, disguised as Arab milkmen, planted six milk-cans of high explosives in the basement of the King David Hotel in Jerusalem, housing both British Army Headquarters and the offices of the High Commission. An entire wing of the building was demolished and a hundred and ten bodies, mostly British, were found among the debris.

In seven months four different solutions were announced, and a new conference convened by Bevin met sixty times to seek a compromise. Agreement was out of the question, and the conference, which opened in London on 10 September 1946, could claim only one distinction: neither of the interested parties would attend and the United States (whose President had publicly affirmed his support for the Zionists) declined to send a representative.

Exhausted by fruitless effort, the Foreign Secretary decided to retreat from the hornets' nest into which he had rushed. On a raw February afternoon in 1947, bitter with disillusion, from the dispatch box in the House of Commons, he announced that Her Majesty's Government would lay the problem before the United Nations.

The United Nations drew its own investigators from eleven countries with no personal interest in Palestine. The Jewish Agency welcomed the visitors and presented its case with skill. The Arab Council bluntly refused to confer. This was nothing new but curiously unwise, and deprived the Arabs of the opportunity to influence events.

On 31 August 1947 the commission of inquiry submitted what amounted to two reports, for its members had been

unable to agree. Seven recommended that Palestine be parti-
tioned into two economically-united states, with Jerusalem and
the surrounding area internationalized and administered under
United Nations control. The other four advocated a federal state
with an Arab province and a Jewish province.

The partition scheme was a geographical aberration in which
each state would have three sectors, whose borders would join
once or not at all. The Jews would have a finger of land hemmed
in by Syria, the Lebanon and two Arab territories on the eastern
border of Galilee, a ninety-mile coastal strip constricted in several
places to barely six miles; and a triangular desert waste in the
Negev. The Arabs would occupy the other half of Galilee wedged
between two Jewish sectors, Samaria and the hills of Judea without the Jerusalem enclave; and a coastal strip barely four miles
deep near Gaza. Over half of the land allocated to the Jews
was owned by Arabs, who were outnumbered by only a thousand
or so, while there were over a hundred thousand Jews living in
those areas proposed for the Arabs.

Accepted by the Jews as the better of two evils but predictably
rejected by the Arabs, the plan, for all its imperfections, was the
most realistic effort so far attempted to separate communities with
nothing in common but their irreconciliability. Its chief, if not
its only merit, after so long, lay in its existence. No small advantage to the fifty-two members of the United Nations before
whom it was laid, and indeed to the whole waiting world. For
the people whose future was at issue it was the signal for a war
whose first victory established the State of Israel on 14 May
1948.

Surrounded by floodlights, Soliman's ramparts looked like a fairy
castle. By the main post office were two Jordanian policemen, with
black uniforms and black helmets. The avenue Salah-ed-Din
(Saladin) was lined with dark, shuttered shops and an abandoned
Turkish house whose tiled roof had been shelled open in the
1948 campaign. It had once belonged to the Nusseibehs, one of
the great Palestinian families of Jerusalem. The American Colony

Hotel was once an Arab palace, and is still renowned for its vast domed rooms and its miraculously perfumed garden. The Arab valet recognized me.

'*Marhaba!*' he cried. 'My friend!' and took my hand and clung to it.

Mr Safieh, a Christian Palestinian, once a member of the Jordanian National Assembly and now the hotel's book-keeper, embraced me as if I were the returning prodigal.

'Welcome! Welcome! How wonderful to see you!'

'How are things with you and your family?'

'All right,' he said, but with a sigh.

Jerusalem is incomparable in spring sunshine, and the garden was a riot of colour and scent. The Staffords, a Quaker couple from Chicago, arrived on a pilgrimage in 1850 after losing their six children and barely surviving a storm in the Atlantic. Beside themselves with grief, they settled in Jerusalem, where in time they produced a second family almost as big as the first. Mrs Stafford founded the first children's hospital in Jerusalem. It still exists, and a sheet from the hospital was used as a white flag when the Turks surrendered the city to the British in 1917. Fifteen other Chicago families followed the Staffords and settled nearby. Today the charming hotel belongs to the great-grandson of the valiant Mrs Stafford.

The same shoeblack worked behind his stool under the orange trees, tall, thin and austere, he had a touch of magic that casually makes the oldest, shabbiest leather shine like glass. He honoured me with a smile.

I like to make contact with Jerusalem from a distance; to edge round before plunging into the complex, spendid city; to watch it in the pink, dusty haze of morning from the windows of the Intercontinental Hotel, which the Jordanians built on the Mount of Olives with gravestones from the old Jewish cemetery spread out below. The silver dome of the El Aqsa mosque tops the Wailing Wall, set back a little from the dome of the rock from which Mohammed took off for heaven. In the distance, higher than the Russian basilica, are the towers of Notre Dame de France, built in the nineteenth century by French Catholics to dominate the schismatic might of Imperial Russia.

Emile Safieh was calm, kindly and stocky, with bright blue eyes, always dressed in European clothes: a typical Christian Arab. He was a good deal less well-off in the Jewish Occupation for, apart from being a member of the National Assembly, he had once owned a small travel agency. Today the majority of travellers were American Jews who naturally preferred Jewish agencies.

He and his family lived in a modern house behind the American colony. The drawing-room, with one ceiling-light, was packed with reproduction furniture. Mrs Safieh was suffused with melancholy warmth, buxom, pretty but heavy, and she immediately produced nuts, almond cakes and little chocolate fancies, recounting meanwhile the story of the hunger strike which she and other Palestinian ladies had staged at the Holy Sepulchre to protest at the detention of Arab women who had been arrested after a series of bomb outrages in the occupied territories. It was hard not to smile at the thought of dear, chubby, sweet-toothed Mrs Safieh settling down for a day on the flagstones of the Holy Sepulchre. A friend at the consulate told me that the ladies sustained themselves with coffee-breaks every two hours.

Mrs Safieh's account of her harrowing ordeal was continually interrupted by her daughter Diana, a plump, pretty girl with wildly immoderate views. She had talked 'Mummy' into the hunger strike and gave us diatribes against the Zionists, accusing them of systematic torture on a scale which made the Gestapo seem like nursemaids. The Arabs were united in their determination to resist. Another plate of *petits fours* was passed. Arab living-conditions were appalling; Jews insisted on the payment of taxes, and even compelled people to put their rubbish in communal dustbins; in the old days a man came to the house to take away the rubbish. Al Fatah had certainly not blown up the Swiss air-liner; 'they' had hushed everything up because the plane had been chock-full of Jewish arms and ammunition. I listened, dazed and increasingly exhausted; nothing bores me quite so much as hate.

Miss Assia Halaby arrived, a fifty-five-old spinster, clothed (rather than dressed) in a flannel suit at the sleeves of which she picked nervously; with her youthful, frizzy grey hair carelessly piled into a bun, she resembled a caricature of an English governess. She was the only Arab woman to have attained the rank of major in the British army, and until she retired in 1948 had supervised a vehicle depot.

There had been Jewesses with her in the army; some were even officers, but she had never talked to them. They tried to tack on to her, hoping to advance their careers, and their sly tricks had lost her her first chance of a commission. They were quite despicable here, seizing houses and picking them dry so that afterwards nothing was left, not even her school-books.

The British military had settled in her memory as superior, inaccessible beings, and to live in their shadow would be the most enviable of fates. Such anglomania is infused into far corners of the Empire, even where the battle for independence has been hardest, so that you will see an Indian officer with a swagger cane and an Oxford accent; or a Jordanian soldier, dressed in British battle-dress, his hand like a cabbage leaf, saluting Hussein. How could those strange, stiff military men, sometimes stupid, often admirable, obsessed with 'class' and 'breeding', hypnotize countless races often subtler or older than their own?

The King David Hotel is a haven for Americans – Jewish tourists, ornate, unnaturally fair ladies and gentlemen stabbing ten-inch cigars. A group of journalists were clustering round Jules Dassin and Melina Mercouri on their second day in Israel. Dassin kept a pastel-coloured eye on his wife, younger in the flesh than on celluloid. From her somewhat agitated contribution, it appeared she loved the Virgin but 'physically rejected Israel'. Fortunately a bewildered silence followed this sententious inspiration. Nearby stood George Weidenfeld, the London publisher, suddenly become *Sir* George, his Establishment utterance strangely at odds with his Germanic intonation. Dark, beautiful, scented, be-jewelled, minked, far readier to talk than to listen, Marion Javits is wife of the Republican senator for New York. David Samuel, the grandson of Sir Herbert Samuel, first British gover-nor of Palestine, detached us from the Dassins and took us to the Finks. Finks is the Lipp of Jewish Jerusalem. Here we sat hemmed in by chairs clustered so close round the little tables that we almost sat on one another's lap. The proprietor, with his square head and flaxen hair, might have been a Frankfurt law-yer. His smile reflected minutely the current status or market-value of a customer. David Samuel got top rating from ear to ear. He has an impeccable Oxford accent and is a biochemist at the Weizmann Institute, engaged in research into the chemistry of memory. He talked about the liaison between the Jewish and Palestinian communities. He had once been worried about Al Fatah ('Guerrillas always win in the end'), but was less so now.

He heard me decry the ugliness of Tel Aviv, and told me that his grandfather had first erected five houses there, round about 1920, as accommodation for the new immigrants. No one had ever supposed that that mosquito-ridden strip of sand would become a city. Now it is too late, and Tel Aviv with its five hundred thousand inhabitants is condemned to ugli-ness. 'We lacked imagination,' Samuel confessed.

From the *Jerusalem Post* I learned that two hundred and fifty Jewish families had volunteered to settle in Hebron, a town of forty thousand inhabitants, and one of the largest in the heart of occupied West-Bank Jordan. The story was not especially im-portant. The military occupation of Hebron had gone quite smoothly so far. The people were friendly and the mayor, Sheikh el-Jabaari, quietly helpful, even inviting Israeli journalists to cover the pilgrims' departure for Mecca, which in other occupied towns is unheard of. Coachloads of tourists visit the magnificent mosque, buying pottery, taking snapshots of the little donkey standing in the square, or of peasants posing beside the fountain in long black dresses, and go away feeling exotic and adventurous.

The Israeli government had moved two hundred and fifty Jewish families into this haven of peace on the grounds that Jews had lived in Hebron from time immemorial until the Arab pogrom of 1929. It was high time, proclaimed the *Jerusalem Post*, that they were restored to their rightful home. The initiative was part of an overall plan to settle Jewish communities in the occupied territories, creating a *de facto* state which would have to be taken into account in any later peace-treaty. The placid Arab population had been roused by news of the move, and bombs and grenades had exploed in the town of Abraham.

Samuel Toledano, the Minister for Arab Affairs, told me that the volunteers were recruited without exception from the Orthodox Jews of Mea-Shearim. They would arrive complete with black hats and curl-papers. These Jews of Mea-Shearim are an exceptionally pious community of about four thousand. The men wear a ringlet of hair on either side of their faces, and the women wear turbans over their shaven heads. Separate from other Jews (who are inclined to treat them with derision), they refused to recognize the State of Israel, claiming that Israel is a spiritual concept and cannot be a temporal power. No phantom nation can make demands, and so, in such matters as military service, they granted themselves dispensation. They were mostly shop-keepers in the narrow streets of their native quarter.

If Hebron needed Jewish re-population, why not pick people who knew the Arabs and were familiar with their language and customs? Orthodox Jews can barely tolerate one another. Toledano agreed with a thin smile that the policy was not sensible, and that holding the occupied territories would provide a way of dealing with two separate and impenetrable communities. Having to hand them back might mean one more pogrom.

The explosions in Hebron were only part of a general unrest, and the Israeli authorities had imposed a severe curfew. I was advised to keep away; but, having no tourist camera, I tended to be taken for an Israeli, and I ignored my friends' advice, planning to see Hebron but to travel with a well-disposed Arab. Mr Safieh entrusted me to his brother who lived in the Via Dolorosa, close to St Stephen's Gate, where I collected him.

Outside the city, we were in the soft landscape of Palestine, with red hills and terraces of olives and pears and flowering plums. Dry stone sepia walls stand out against green unripe corn, the background broken now and then by the biblical silhouette of a woman draped in a white veil.

Fifteen miles from Jerusalem we passed a road cutting up into the hill on our right. I had taken that road a year before up to the kibbutz of Kfar-Etzion. I had arrived late when a biting wind scurried the clouds over the rocky hills. In front of two concrete bungalows, a young woman with a green scarf tied round her hair was arranging a small bunch of anemones. Further on, a carroty-haired giant in sandals and a short-sleeved shirt was dissecting a snake, an operation which is standard practice among commandos, for troops separated from their bases can sometimes live on such succulent food for days at a time. A baby cried, a second man came by in a bathrobe. Everyone had bathed. It was Friday and the Sabbath would begin in an hour's time. Prefabricated huts roofed with corrugated iron housed unmarried kibbutzniks, like the huts further off that sheltered the sheep and turkeys. Beyond were rows of fig and cypress seedlings.

In 1948 Kfar-Etzion was isolated and surrounded by Arab villages. Ben Gurion regarded such kubbutzim as indispensable pockets of resistance and would not hear of their evacuation. A young Polish survivor of Belsen had given birth to her first son, and her husband (whom she had met in the concentration camp) joined her at the moment the Arabs attacked the kibbutz with tanks. She would not leave with the women and children, but gave them her baby, who was brought up in the old Arab quarter of Jaffa whose occupants had been moved to the concrete-built camp past which I had driven a few minutes earlier. She died with all the men on the last day of the siege.

The boy carried to safety in 1948 showed me the kibbutz. He was twenty-two, with the smile of an angel. In 1967 the children

124

of those parents who died defending the kibbutz land had returned to their own lives at Kfar-Etzion. This boy, young enough to be my son, had never known his mother. He was an officer in the air force, but planned to become an electronics engineer and live permanently on the kibbutz. To him it was a place in Paradise, though the buildings were squalid and the surrounding slopes were barren under the black clouds. A tall, short-haired girl and a second, thinner and wrapped in a khaki flying-jacket, stared at him with yearning eyes. He spoke to them gently and thoughtfully.

I returned, passing a Palestinian refugee camp, now an Arab village like any other with fountains and square chunks of concrete, glowing pink in the sunset. Beyond was Jerusalem.

Today I kept my accounts of Jewish joys and sorrows from my charming Arab host, who was so friendly that, though I have no taste for the white, gold-trimmed satin of the Crypt, I agreed to stop in Bethlehem, where thirty American tourists were talking their heads off in the crypt of the beautiful church with badly damaged icons.

Outside the town among the flowering plum-trees Solomon came to meditate beside the huge pools which once fed water to Jerusalem. A eunuch of a Queen of Ethiopia was baptized at a spring near some Hellenistic ruins. Beyond is a seventeenth-century Turkish *khan,* a low building once used as an inn where pilgrims, horses and merchants' camels rested in a courtyard surrounded by crenellated walls. History tumbles upon itself in the East, leaving a tomb, a wall or tower and sometimes an entire city. It could seem that nothing changes, that even the same women are silhouetted on the same hillsides under the same sky. Hebron is surrounded by houses of golden stone with flat roofs, tall lancet windows, and a profusion of wrought-iron grilles and balconies reminiscent of the architecture of the Ottoman Empire.

The great mosque of Haram el Khalil lies in an Arab, later Byzantine, fortress built by Herod. A *medhin,* a Moslem priest, gave me a green cloth to cover my head and lower part of my face, while he showed us around. Red and white marble mausoleums housed the tombs of Abraham and his aged wife Sarah in the centre of the mosque, with Rebecca and Isaac parked somewhat on one side, behind a grated aperture covered with green and gold silk embroidery. With my friendly Christian Palestinian and my respectful *medhin* I saluted my venerable ancestors in this Byzantine mosque, and it all seemed remarkably simple. The *medhin's* ancestors had arrived in Hebron seven centuries ago, and he had worked in the mosque for thirty years.

Below the fortress was a cluster of stalls with sheepskins, glassware and pottery for the American tourists piling out of coaches, cameras at the ready. We found the potter behind the mosque working his wheel with his foot. I bought some work painted by his children, simple cups like Persian pottery.

Mr Safieh was nervous of being cut off if there was any trouble in the markets, but I wheedled him on.

The entrance to the maze of markets was guarded by a solitary Jordanian policeman. Cheap, gaudy rubbish lay in piles on veils and long black dresses. Stalls were run by men in white turbans or fezzes. There were no tourists, not a single Israeli soldier or civilian. I got some venomous looks. Shafts of blinding sunlight pierced the tight, dark alleys and vaulted passages.

Mr Safieh quickened his stride.

A turbaned Moslem, arrogant by his tiny window, sold me two copper goblets. He smiled when I used my Arabic and gave him *'Salam Alekum'*, a particularly heartfelt farewell. The whole street had been keeping an eye on me and I felt them relax. Luckily further conversation was only thanks and salutations for I had already squandered my stock of Arabic. Skinned sheep lay about, flies buzzing round the entrails drying in the hot sun; next door the heads gazed open-mouthed in some ovine nirvana, while opposite three men carefully scraped the skins. My appetite was gone before we reached the butcher.

Mr Safieh visited a friend while I tried to park the car in a more suitable parking place. This was not easy since I lose all sense of direction when faced by a multitude of no-entry signs. I lost my way. I know only that Mr Safieh's rendezvous was in a chemist's shop. Small, shrill children, taking me for an Israeli, shouted *'Shalom'* and fell in step with me until there were nearly twenty of them. A young man, looking faintly hostile, inquired where I was going. The vagueness of my explanations and my pathetic Arabic vocabulary turned him into a knight-errant, and he led me safely to the chemist's when Safieh's friend, Mr Sharaf, a former deputy at the Jordanian parliament, elegantly draped in a large brown *abaya,* arranged chairs in a ring, and friends, intrigued to see me sipping coffee, trooped in, bowed ceremoniously and joined us. Sharaf had fought at Kfar-Etzion, and I asked him to drive with me one day and describe the battle. He tut-tutted and refused. He was afraid that the Jews would put him in prison. Anyway, he would need a permit.

The only place to eat on the outskirts of town was the Park Hotel of the Eternal Garden, where the proprietor served fried eggs, and Safieh grumbled about the Occupation, taxes, and local rates. You had to pay per cubic foot to have your rubbish removed, which seemed to him unfair, as they taxed people simply because they had large houses. Rubbish-removal seemed to be a major bone of contention, and Teddy Kolek, the mayor of Jerusalem, had been obliged to state, in reply to sharp questioning from Moslem deputies, that the Jewish city corporation drew no distinction between Jewish rubbish and Arab rubbish.

Mr Safieh continued vehemently about the road-tax, the cost of motor insurance at twenty-three pounds a year, the increase of wages by thirty per cent, which saddled employers with social-insurance contributions, land tax, and income tax. He admitted that they rarely paid these taxes and were rarely pressed for settlement, but that was because of the authorities' canniness and desire to avoid incidents. They would certainly be pressed if the Jews retained Jerusalem under a peace treaty.

A breeze rustled the branches of the olive-trees while Mr Safieh poured out his grievances. He was a good, gentle man and, while the Occupation was not crippling or inhuman, he nevertheless suffered. And in terms of the incalculable value of freedom, who could fail to understand him?

I questioned him with compassion, and he replied with courtesy. Yes, the Arabs in Jerusalem are free to move about, but in the occupied territories they need a permit. You can get one easily enough, but 'they' search your car, though not so often recently. It was true: there were hardly any Israeli police in the village. He never went into modern Jerusalem or Tel Aviv, he would be scared. He knew nothing would happen, but he would be scared. There was no Arab municipal council in Jerusalem, only two deputies. 'They' tried to get Arabs to join, but they refused.

Teddy Kollek was not a bad man, quite humane in fact. He wanted to compensate former Arab landlords, but nothing had come of it, and 'they' wouldn't get much. He did not hate the Jews, but wanted them out of the occupied territories. He didn't believe that three million should be driven into the sea, and even those who had said so didn't really think it. Jews were treated well in Arab countries. There were Iraqi Jews in the Old City who could not wait for the war to end so that they could go back to Iraq. The stories put about were quite untrue, and Jews in Iraq, Egypt and Syria couldn't be treated better.

This remark had me up in arms. He gave way but became vexed. The Jews took everything in '67, homes and cars. He longed to see the back of them! They built an army, which wasn't very difficult, with German reparations and American armaments. He did not admire Nasser, who had had the wrong people around him and should have known the condition of his army. The upheaval had mainly affected the middle classes. The peasants' life hadn't altered much: they tilled their land as they did before.

I asked him carefully about Bedouin indifference to the Occupation. The Bedouins live a good deal better as a result of the Occupation, which has brought electrification of villages, irrigation, provision of fertilizers, and the allocation of funds to pur-

In the golden light of the afternoon, the women of Shakka gather around the fountain, near to a ruined Roman house

Silvery Aleppo with its Moslem seminaries and Mosques bristling with spiky minarets . . .

Jerusalem from the Mount of Olives. The El Aqsa Mosque and the Dome of the Rock can be seen in the foreground. The Wailing Wall stretches out on the left of the picture

At one end of the sunswept *Haram*, an arched colonnade of golden stones overlooking the Armenian quarter

chase farming equipment. They were more inclined to take root than to swell the ranks of Al Fatah.

He agreed, but had high hopes of Al Fatah. Not that he wanted the situation to drag on. Whether an Arab got killed or a Jew got killed, the result was the same, and it made him unhappy. The guerrillas bragged a lot and claimed credit for imaginary exploits, but everyone did that. The only solution was to work out some sort of agreement with the Jews.

A mile or two from Jerusalem was an old Jewish army camp, riddled with bullet-holes, which housed the Ministry of Defence. The view of the sunlit hills was magnificent, but my friend was uneasy and thought it no place to linger.

I watched Safieh's tall, stooping figure recede slowly beneath the high arches of St Stephen's Gate. He loved Jerusalem as passionately as any Jew.

I dolled myself up in a white crêpe dress, challenged by a dinner invitation from Gita Sherover, the doyenne of Jerusalem social life. Her beautiful house in the residential quarter of Rehavia glowed with bougainvilleas and poinsettias and in her drawing-room, surrounded by Chagall, Cross, Utrillo and Renoir, she entertained Israel's leading intellectuals, politicians and generals.

Short, dark, slender, with chiselled features, she had a generous spirit but could be guilty of some remarkably intense and intolerant utterances. Her husband, Miles, needed his tactful command of half a dozen languages to dam up her wilder torrents. He had come from Venezuela and the peaceful existence of a prosperous industrialist. On a visit to Israel he met Gita who won him over to the Zionist cause which she so charmingly embodied. He was a happy acquisition for the country as well, being uncommonly generous and extremely rich. He had just endowed Jerusalem's first full-sized theatre.

Theirs could be the gayest, pleasantest evenings, full of light laughter. As when Dinstein, the strapping ex-deputy finance minister, told us of being stopped for speeding while in his old

Buick. Only the first letter was legible on the bonnet. 'It's a B for Buick,' said the policeman, 'not B for Boeing!'

Ygal Yadin, the archaeologist, told us he had been stopped doing seventy on the road to Tel Aviv and, the formalities having been concluded, the officer said to him, 'You were very good on television last night; you must see our radar system over here, behind the bush. It brings in a lot of money and the government needs every penny now that the French have stopped supplying Mirages. These new Phantoms are very expensive!'

The fast-moving, elliptical conversation turned to Hussein, for whom Gita had no sympathy. 'Nobody, after all, had bothered when he hanged three spies in public in Amman. The newspapers had barely mentioned it.'

Yadin talked of Hussein's grandfather Abdullah, whom he had met in 1948 and had found shrewd and likeable, a *grand seigneur* who had great courage. A true statesman who genuinely wanted a peaceful settlement with Israel, which had cost him his life.

At a preliminary meeting in 1948, Abdullah told the Jewish delegates, "When the enemy is hard on your heels, you cling to your possessions and get caught, or you shed a few from time to time to give your horse a better chance. That is what I am doing.'

It only rankled with Abdullah that the Israelis expected him to treat with a woman; and one day, asking Yadin where Mrs Meir was and hearing she was in Moscow, he had expressed the quizzical wish that she might stay there.

Yadin was less flattering to the former Jordanian commander-in-chief, Abdullah Tell.* They had driven together through Jericho to meet with the king, a tumultuous journey during which crowds of Arabs, brandishing rifles, brought the car to a standstill. During this escapade Abdullah Tell confided to Yadin that the king wished to 'liberate and unify' the Lebanon, Syria and Jordan and have them all under his control, and would be

---

* In the end, Abdullah Tell betrayed the king. He was sentenced to death in his absence for being party to the conspiracy which led to Abdullah's murder. The Protection of his cousin Wasfi Tell, the Jordanian prime minister, enabled him to return to Amman in recent years. Wasfi Tell was himself assassinated in Cairo in November 1971.

glad of Jewish help in the enterprise. He had asked for three planes, which they would repaint and hit Damascus with before Damascus knew what had hit it. Yadin didn't tell us his answer to the Arab commander, but added wryly that three planes had then been the entire Jewish air force.

A journalist of *The Times* was eager to know Yadin's estimate of Glubb Pasha, the British commander of the Arab legion who had caused the Haganah such serious trouble.

'Glubb certainly knew how to handle "the Arabs", as he called his Bedouin troops. The Jews wouldn't let him take part in the talks, as they didn't want the decision to be laid at Britain's door. Glubb wasn't a particularly good military leader; he lacked flair. Many of his laurels were due to the efforts of three first-rate British officers in the Arab Legion. Actually, King Abdullah seemed tired of Glubb Pasha and his high-handed ways.'

'And wasn't he surprised by the speed of the campaign in 1967?'

'Everyone was, apart from people with access to intelligence reports. The captured Egyptian battle-plan was a pretty good one, but it was a plan of attack, not of defence. Their planes were all set to take off, which is why they weren't hidden away inside hangars. Had they attacked they would have been over Tel Aviv in four minutes and things might have gone either way. Even taking an optimistic view of the outcome, the campaign would have been longer, harder and far more costly in terms of casualties. You know,' said Yadin, 'I really can't imagine why we grumble. We are so much safer than in '67 when we had either to attack or be destroyed.'

A slightly-built American joined us, looking about forty and as supple as a ballet dancer, with blazing eyes, grey, unruly hair and an electrifying personality. Everyone greeted him with enthusiasm. He wore the *'canapé'* of a Commander of the Legion of Honour and knew everyone. He might have been the ambassador of some free and easy country. After he had left I learnt that this captivating figure was Leonard Bernstein, who was giving concerts in Israel.

I tucked into a plateful of chicken and almonds worthy of Canton
(where Gita's cook came from). Samuel Toledano, the Minister
for Arab Affairs, told me he had spoken Arabic at home and that
many of his childhood friends were Arabs, whom he saw frequently. They were lawyers, teachers, doctors, and often came to
his house with his Jewish friends.

He talked of the number of volunteers needed and the problems of bringing the two communities closer together. For instance, an Arab woman from the occupied territories acquired
Israeli citizenship by marriage to an Israeli Arab. A large number
of Arabs would slip over to Gaza to buy wives for two hundred
pounds sterling, one fifth of their price in Israel; one Bedouin
chief buying fifteen wives in Gaza made fifteen new citizens
who in ten years would be a hundred little Israeli Arabs. Exit
visas were easy, but the Jordanians, not wanting an Arab majority,
would turn their owners back at the frontier, having enough
trouble with their own Palestinian refugees.

Gita was trying to draw me into a conversation with a small,
elderly gentleman holding forth with obvious self-satisfaction and
a German accent which rather got on my nerves. He was Nahum
Goldman, the president of the World Jewish Congress, whose
plan to visit Cairo to discuss peace with Nasser had been vetoed
by Golda Meir. But Toledano was more interesting on the fate
of the Palestinians. They had suffered for twenty-five years.
They were highly-developed people, many of whom had studied
at European universities. Often they lost their homes in neigh-
bourhoods like Katamon and Bakaa and other sites earmarked
for blocks of flats to accommodate new immigrants. It was sad
to see them taking a last look at their old homes. Naturally
they would be compensated. But they wouldn't accept the 1948
prices they had been offered by the Government. The value of
the properties has risen steeply since then, and they were demanding the full current market price. This was just as unreasonable,
as the new value was due to the new roads and facilities like
running water, electricity and the telephone. Even an intermediate
1956 valuation, with interest at three per cent, would cost the

state a hundred and fifty million dollars. The problem also existed in Haifa and Jaffa, and the whole Tel Aviv sea-front used to belong to Arabs. Obviously they could not return; everything had changed so much. Often the original owner had died, and his heirs might be scattered all over the world, each entitled to a claim. How could the problem ever be solved, when the number of Palestinian refugees was over a million and a half? No amount of financial compensation would ever satisfy them. On the other hand, how could a million and a half refugees be absorbed in an area defined in 1948 as eight thousand square miles.

Notre Dame de France rises like a great barn in the south-east corner of Jerusalem, overlooking the city walls and the Jaffa Gate. Still gaping from a cannon-ball of the 1948 campaign, it belongs to the Assumptionists, of whom only six remain. They tried to sell it to the Karen Kayemet, the Jewish National Fund, for the Hebrew University, for the tidy sum of six hundred thousand dollars, but the Vatican has opposed the deal.

Miss Halaby, the retired Palestinian British army major whom I had met at the Safiehs, was showing me her Jerusalem: streets of red-tiled houses, some ripped open by shells; stretches of waste ground, and a few modest building-sites. Some streets were lively, with children playing hopscotch, with mothers wheeling prams, and tiny gardens of dustbins, shabby lean-to's, old tyres, a few hens, and an occasional rose-bush. This former Arab quarter close to the old Mandelbaum Gate, which marked the frontier between Israel and Jordan until the Six-Day War, was now inhabited by Jews, to the anger and disgust of my guide.

'All Arab property,' the poor woman sighed. 'No sooner had the Jews moved in than the neighbourhood disappeared under a sea of orange-peel, banana-skins, great piles of rubbish whichever way you looked!!'

The Mandebaum Gate is now a substantial terrace where a small pile of stones holds a bullet-holed helmet, a submachine-gun, and a Hebrew inscription.

'Murderers!' hissed Miss Halaby, glowering at a lovely young creature in a mini-skirt. That one should live to see such abomination in our beloved Jerusalem!'

With an irate gesture, she straightened the black woollen bonnet which had begun to relinquish hold on her grey hair, and we entered the Old City.

In the afternoon I saw the other half of the picture. Iacov Tsur, who had once represented the Israeli government in Paris, offered to show me 'his' Jerusalem and took me to Yemin Moshe, the Jewish quarter founded by a wealthy Englishman, Sir Moses Montefiore, in 1838. His wife, who made the journey with him, was torn between wonder at the beauty of the Old City and terror of the plague with which the area was stricken. In her journal she wrote:

> As we drew nearer to Jerusalem the aspect of the surrounding country became more and more sterile and gloomy. The land was covered with thorns and briers . . . melancholy desolateness of the rocky hills and valleys . . . for now the Holy City itself rose full into view, with all its cupolas and minarets reflecting the splendour of the heavens . . . The pure air of the Mount of Olives breathed around us with the most refreshing fragrance . . . We are, however, persuaded not to enter (the city) cases of plague having occurred . . . It is, therefore our determination to remain . . . on this beautiful mount where the finest air, the most sublime views and associations of the noblest kind unite to comfort us and elevate our thoughts . . . The chief cause of the plague is extreme poverty, and Mrs Y told me she had seen people eating the grass and weeds from excess of hunger.

Sir Moses bought these hills and valleys from the Arabs, and in this afflicted setting he started to build the first Jewish quarter outside the walls of the Old City, away from the poverty and squalor. It is a quiet, peaceful neighbourhood, with short bushy trees on the corners of the streets, and an incongruous windmill, donated by Montefiore, which adds a touch of Holland to architectural features from almost everywhere else.

The new immigrants were afraid of attack by starving Bedouins, and as an inducement to live there Sir Moses offered a pound sterling every night to every pioneer bold enough to stay outside the walls. It worked.

These charming, gently-proportioned houses were due for demolition. Space was short, and homes had to be found for the continuing inflow of Jews. The government was determined that Jerusalem should be a Jewish city, and had planned a grey belt of high-rise, low-rent flats capable of absorbing three hundred thousand new citizens. The mayor, Teddy Kollek, had opposed the plan, repelled by the idea that, having survived so much, Jerusalem should be systematically polluted, debased and made ugly. But he had to bow to prevailing conditions, and acknowledge that one cannot 'build towns in the country.'*

The Yemenite quarter was poorer, with the narrow streets full of yelling, boisterous children. An old man with a grey beard and a black skullcap wrapped with a white turban showed us the tiny synagogue, a single, square-shaped room with a bulb hanging from the ceiling, a few wooden benches, and the Torah, a neatly wrapped bundle, set in a corner.

We spoke to everyone; old women gossiped merrily and wished us *mazel tov,* good luck.

The prosperous Jewish colony of Bukhara, on the borders of Uzbekistan and Turkmenistan, the southern marches of Holy Russia, was made up of well-to-do merchants who imported silks and spices from India and China and wove splendid rich red carpets for the western world. They were driven out by the pogroms of the late ninetenth century and flocked to Jerusalem. Their quarter, with its houses and quiet wide streets, was a striking contrast to the one we had just left. We called on a wealthy merchant and his dark, plump, soft-eyed daughters, who showed us the sumptuous brocade dresses they wore at special family functions and their treasure of Bukhara fabrics, including an artless eighteenth-century scene from

*Alphonse Allais.

the Old Testament with an inscription in dubious Hebrew.

Ehon Moshe is Jerusalem's Sephardic quarter, and I was curious, as I come from one of those families which settled in Spain and lived through the golden age of the tenth and eleventh centuries. Uprooted by the Inquisition in 1492, they scattered along the Mediterranean. Some came to Palestine, bringing their liberal traditions and wide-ranging culture, forming active, highly-developed, often intellectual enclaves in Jerusalem as elsewhere. Their numbers were increased by Sephardim from North Africa after the French withdrawal, and by Iraqi and Yemenite Jews for whom life became intolerable after 1948.

These two later groups are proletariat, providing a human reservoir to open up intractable deserts like Negev and Sharm-el-Sheik. Though the war has had a levelling effect, the Sephardim from Africa and Asia still hold second place in Israel and their discontent is particularly among the young, whose groups, like the Black Panthers, mount unrestrained and sometimes savage demonstrations.

The houses were Spanish in style, with delicate colours and overhanging balconies, but the paintwork was peeling and the roofs were repaired with corrugated iron. A twelve-year-old boy playing with his scooter came from Morocco, but he couldn't remember where.

The adjoining quarter is Mahana-Jehuda, Judah's Camp, with a market as large and busy as the Old City, narrow streets and stalls sagging with oranges, strawberries, vegetables, and bright fabrics. The crowd was solely Jewish, with only two Arab women in brown robes and white veils selling vegetables to the passers-by. The pastry-stores were as rich as the Arab stalls in the Old City; but the Jewish flies were less lucky, the delicacies being protected by plastic. No desiccated sheep here, where the butchers were Kosher and the animals were killed and bled strictly according to the law. Chickens were ritually slaughtered by five young men in black skullcaps, in line at a bench in a spacious shop on the main street. They hold a small silver knife in their teeth while they take a chicken, and, turning the head and flattening the stray feathers on its neck, make one effortless incision. The chicken hangs head-down in an opening hollowed in the end of the bench, and in minutes the blood has drained out as the law demands. The young men did three thousand chickens a day, and their speed and skill were not cruel or repulsive.

At a cocktail-party that evening I had my first unpleasant social experience, when Mr Avigda of the local radio station treated me in a peremptory and omniscient tone to a lecture on de Gaulle, France's policy, the arms embargo, and sundry allied subjects. My impression was that the proud anger of the year following the embargo had now, with the Israelis' disappointment in Pompidou, become an overt and bitter resentment. There was no mistaking the attitude of the man in the street. When young hitch-hiking soldiers heard me speak French, they scowled, and retired into their shells. When I asked for directions in English, people were extremely courteous and helpful, but when I said I came from Paris their attitude changed, and one man muttered a curt 'Oh!' and turned his back on me.

I caught the last programme at the Zion Cinema in Jaffa Road in the New City's business centre. The shabby auditorium has noisy wooden seats and was full of young soldiers and their girl-friends, all very quiet and well-behaved. Before the main feature and in the interval there were short films on cleanliness. Fruit-skins must be placed in dustbins, not thrown on the ground; hands must be washed, feet wiped, houses cleaned, flowers and fruit-trees planted. These points were made with simple light-hearted images and I thought of Miss Halaby and her long-drawn-out complaint about the new immigrants and 'rubbish whichever way you looked'.

Piero Founi drove me north to the hills and valleys on the Syrian and Lebanese borders, Flavius Josephus's blessed land of Galilee.

We were to visit the kibbutz home of Ehud Avriel, the former

Israeli ambassador to Italy and, in Ben Gurion's words, 'one or the four begetters of the State of Israel'. He was a tubby man with clear, melancholy, kind eyes. His natural warmth had a hint of reserve, neither disdainful nor aloof, but reflecting an unquenchable inner life. He seemed to understand everything with a lightning intuition and a remarkable deductive intellect.

We left the coastal plain with its odd patchwork of orange plantations and built-up areas, and stopped briefly at Meggido. One of the chief archaeological sites in Israel, it has traces of the Neolithic, the Sumerian, the Canaanite, the Pharaonic and the Philistine. The crusaders made their contribution, and so did General Allenby in 1918, when he encircled the Turks and earned himself the title of Viscount Allenby of Meggido.

It is a good dig with plenty of helpful signs, but nothing to compare with Ur, though it has a nobility of its own, turned slightly oppressive by heavy clouds rumbling over Solomon's stables like a stampeding pack of horses. Labourers from Tyre built the stables in the tenth century B.C., and though there is little left of them but a few bits of walls, we could almost hear the whinnyings of the six-score royal steeds, and the rolling thunder and the clatter of hooves in the cobbled drives, and the wind-whipped yellow marguerites under the wall of the stable-master's house. Not even palm-trees, grown up through the battered ramparts, can calm this tormented place. It has witnessed too many wars and sieges, passions and turmoils, lives and deaths. People were bellowing: not envoys of Pharaoh, but emissaries, alas, of the American diaspora, aged between eight and eighty. I fled.

The rectangular concrete of the kibbutzim clung to the hills, which were downy with apple, pear, olive and plum trees in pink and white blossom. Kibbutzniks walked or cycled in shorts and jeans, the ubiquitous small linen hats sheltering their eyes from the blazing sun. They greeted us with cheerful waves.

The pioneers of the kibbutzim had everything against them. Galilee was covered with marshes plagued by mosquitoes and fever. The kibbutzniks planted eucalyptus which grew quickly and sucked up the water. The same trees are now huge and venerable, dappled with white, and their long perfumed leaves quivered in the breeze. Undrained marshes were tamed as reservoirs for irrigation: the hard pressed pioneers had the rich soil from a maze of basaltic stone, and now the valleys are covered with a green spread of tobacco, cereals, and even cotton.

A fair young man with a bushy moustache told us with discreet but unmistakable respect that Ehud Avriel's house was 'the stone one, not the wooden one standing next to it'.

Avriel received us in a simply-furnished room, surrounded by as many books as the walls would hold. A stentorian giant of a man was precariously accommodated in an armchair. Whimsical and humorous, he was an R.A.F. air ace of the Second World War, and still retained a slight hint of craziness. Avriel was as friendly as ever: considerate, incisive, impressive. In his heroic, romantic past, he had master-minded the struggling of immigrants at the end of the European war, and the supplying of arms to the Haganah. His adventures had been worthy of James Bond.

He was Israel's first ambassador in Prague, delegate to the conference of African States in Accra, and finally – as a reward for past services – ambassador to Italy. He now lives a quiet unassuming life, and his wife manages a tourist hotel in the kibbutz.

Many Israelis, having played their part, retire to this kind of simple, austere, rural life. In Ehud's case this was only one side of the coin; he travelled to Tel Aviv several times a week and was often abroad. The telephone rang frequently and, although he spoke Hebrew, I could tell from his calm voice that doors were opening, details being settled and contacts formed or reestablished.

'You must go and see Ben Gurion,' he urged us as he shepherded us along the shaky, flower-bordered path to the kibbutz restaurant. It was a self-service restaurant with full-length windows overlooking the green landscape, serving *hors d'oeuvre,* meat, potatoes, vegetables, oranges, and either water or beer. At the end of the meal you took your plate and cutlery to the three kibbutzniks on dining-room duties that month.

Some of the small wooden houses among the bordered paths had pretty gardens and were well cared for. Others were an eyesore.

'One does one's best to influence and persuade, but I'm sorry to say the younger members are often the worst offenders. They don't realize the sweat and toil and sacrifice that went into making all this.'

I had heard this complaint against the young Israelis before. They had never watched a tree emerging inch by inch from harsh soil; they were blind to the thrill of corn ripening in a field wrested from the desert; they took everything for granted and cared little for the wooden houses in the kibbutz, never having lived in tents with mosquitoes swarming. Their sights, anyway, were set on an apartment in Tel Aviv or Haifa.

Ehud told us about his younger daughter, who had been conscripted for military service and was stationed at Kiryat-Shmonah, a small market-town six miles from the kibbutz and uncomfortably close to Syria and the Lebanon. It was often shelled, and ambushes were common in the roads in and out of the town. The Avriels had two Jewish guests from New York, and took them to a concert in Kiryat-Shmonah to show them how life went on regardless of danger. They met their daughter with her commanding officer, and all had a meal together afterwards. They were nibbling their kebabs when a soldier told the commanding officer that he was needed urgently in Haifa. He gave Avriel's daughter the keys of the jeep, and apologized for being unable to see her back to camp. At one o'clock in the morning the girl would have to drive twenty miles on a road almost within hailing distance of the Syrian border. Her anguished parents, fearful of a guerrilla ambush, kissed her and returned silently to the kibbutz with their American guests. Suddenly the American woman remarked to her husband in the nasal tones of her Brooklyn home, 'Honey, do you realize in this country it's safe for a girl to go home alone after midnight?'

It was sad to say goodbye to friends who live so far away and whom you may never see again.

Ehud was firmly against our plan to drive alongside the Syrian border to the Golan heights, and urged us to make straight for Safad after Quneitra and to keep away from the frontier road, where two soldiers had been ambushed the night before. We promised not to get out of the car, for the roadsides had not been cleared of mines since 1967.

The scenery changed abruptly from the green, fertile fields of Galilee to the austere Druze country; behind us was the great snowclad cone of Mount Hermon, where Israeli skiers practise on their side of the nine-thousand feet heights. The hills became mountains, the valleys wide plateaux, and instead of crops there were tough shrubs of broom and thorns. The road through the black basalt rocks was fringed with poppies and tall weeds, and it was hard to imagine the hidden menace of unexploded mines. Occasional barbed-wire entanglements and death's-head signboards appeared, but we seemed to be entirely alone. For several hundred yards the road followed the first narrow thread of the Jordan trickling into a rocky defile. Soon we reached the square, flat-roofed stone houses of the Druze village, where the women were in bright skirts and black bodices, with long veils drawn in a straight line across their foreheads, and the men in white *keffiehs* encircled by black *aguils;* they waved cheerfully at us. An ancient, white-bearded man passed on a donkey with four or five young women following behind. The Israeli Druzes are first cousins to the Syrian Druzes and the Druzes of the Golan border district. They are a minority group and, although deeply religious, have no places of worship. The Syrians ignore them or treat them as poor and rather dubious relations, but the Israelis have been more generous or more shrewd, and the Syrian Druzes who held the impregnable Golan heights in 1967 abandoned their positions after offering only token resistance to the Israeli Druzes.

In Quneitra, a grey, sprawling Syrian market-town, there were two men and one donkey and that was all. Every house was ripped open, many of the roofs had been shelled, and a large white hospital, several storeys high, gaped windowless at the baleful wreckage of the sheikh's palace, the façade of the Syrian army camp, and the prefabricated barracks, were charred and riddled with shrapnel. There was no sign of people or animals, just the wind bending the grasses.

Israeli soldiers were billeted in small whitewashed houses on the far side of Quneitra. There were a lot of them, and jeeps and half-tracks everywhere, and the remains of Russian-built Molotova tanks sticking out of ditches along the road winding from plateau to plateau.

A sharp turn, and we found the half-buried site of an ancient town and could make out among the poppies and marguerites a fragment of a Roman arch and some Canaanite stones. The road sloped down to a hump-backed bridge over the mighty Jordan (still just a puny greenish brooklet). Looking back to the Syrian bank were the deeply-embedded camouflaged blockhouses, from which Syrian troops had raked the kibbutzim in the Galilean plain. There were more Israeli camps. The sky turned grey, the Jordan surged through the dark gorges, and the rain hit us.

Friday is the chief day of prayer for Moslems and marks the beginning of the Jewish Sabbath. And so Good Friday is three times blessed in the Old City.

I made for the Via Dolorosa wedged between the old city hospital and a small Polish museum. It curves narrowly between yellow walls marked with the Stations of the Cross, leaving on its left the convent of Our Lady of Sion, towards which I ambled gaily in the mild early-morning sunlight. I heard a choir and suddenly saw coming towards me a slow procession of gaudy ties and flower-trimmed hats. I was flattened like a swatted fly against the cold, smooth wall, and it filled me with wonder and an odd sense of the absurd to hear these too, too solid Anglo-Saxons intoning with soulful heartiness the mournful hymn 'Only Your Blood, Jesus'. They surged past, and it wasn't funny but very moving, for behind the flowery matrons came every age and race and class and colour, even a loping black giant in a white baseball cap. French pilgrims followed, and once more I pressed against the wall. Black-suited priests led a substantial group who didn't sing, which was just as well, because French singing, regardless of the words, is apt to come out like a rather maudlin street-ballad. The priest faced his pilgrims and delivered a fine homily on Christ who had shouldered his cross joyfully. The cross was the symbol of human life with its torments and responsibilities, and the message of the Passion was that life, too, should be shouldered joyfully.*

After the French came the Spaniards, in black serried ranks of soutanes and mantillas. Men, shadowed in mourning, bent under the weight of a huge ebony cross. From the folds of their mourning, women thrust out plump hands with bright painted fingernails. A very beautiful young girl, also in black, mimed helping the men with their burden, without taking her eyes off a handsome priest whose responding glance seemed hardly ecclesiastical. He painted Christ's sufferings in colours like Goya – full of blood, terror and tears.

A growing rumble came from the throng packed in the narrow street, a growl of wrath and exasperation beyond any response to an event two thousand years old. It was as if the Crucifixion was the symbol of all the cruelties and terror in the modern world. But how deeply would the cruelty and terror touch these monks who fingered the cross like a fetish? They cursed the murderers of Christ and began a doleful hymn as they moved along the street. The final group was a motley band of smiling nuns, young tourists in mauve mini-skirts, venerable Arabs in white *keffiehs* and a few small grey donkeys. An Arab was trying to sell films to an elderly American woman in pink. 'No, no thank you, I don't need any,' she told him. Need any? *He* neeeded a living. He continued to pester her and she began to look slightly

---

* I am reminded of a pithy quotation from Malraux: 'What is the use of your learning to play the lyre, Socrates, since you are going to die?' 'I shall have learned to play the lyre before I die.'

afraid. 'I told you I don't want any!' she cried, pushing him away. And then they were gone, swept away by the tide.

I began to feel oppressed and deafened, and threaded my way towards the Haram, the large esplanade around the Dome of the Rock and the El-Aqsa mosque whose gold and silver cupolas hover in the blue sky.

The calm of the sun-swept esplanade was almost physical after the tumult of the Old City; it was like plunging into the sea. Within this trapezium the ancient Hebrews conferred with Yahweh. Today the Dome of the Rock is the third religious sanctuary of Moslem world after Mecca and Medina. Solomon and Omar walked here, as did Herod and the Roman legions, the Frankish kings and the Templars. The Dome stands at the very centre of the Esplanade, eight-sided with glazed tiling and topped with a golden cupola. The mark of the hand of the archangel Gabriel is imprinted on the rock where he held it down to prevent it from following Mahommed to heaven. The dome of the El-Aqsa Mosque glints aluminium in the background. The light is clear and soft; a gentle breeze plucks the scarlet roses round the yews and grass; wild flowers spring up between the flagstones.

Below the esplanade an Arab student recited his lesson, striding among the buttercups. Farther off, a peasant on a tractor worked among the olive trees. Around the Cedron valley, the hills were washed blue with morning. By now there was a note of frenzy in the student's self-instruction. At the edge of the esplanade, in the arched porch of a little white house topped by an oblate cupola, a man in a chestnut *arabaya* and a gleaming white turban sat on a small wooden stool, praying aloud, his eyes closed, his face burnished in the gentle sun. Rows of pointed arches, each different in design, framed glimpses of landscape like fifteenth-century primitives.

Ever since an Australian called Rohan (subsequently declared insane) tried to burn the El Aqsa down, there had been Jordanian policemen to prevent non-Arabs from entering. Among other dramatic incidents here was the assassination in 1947 of Abdullah

of Jordan, slain by a Palestinian who thought him over-submissive
to Britain and disloyal to the cause of Arab independence.

At the south end of the esplanade is the imposing building
which, until the thirteenth century, was the residence of the
Grand Master of the Order of Templars. Around were Arab
traders gossiping in guttural tones, and women who had laid
down their baskets and stood in a glittering circle, exchanging
confidences. Even the Jordanian guardians were deep in conversation with traders at the Maghrebins Gate. Two Jewish soldiers
walked by, a girl with a pony-tail swinging beneath her forage
cap and a short skirt hugging her hips and thighs, and a boy,
tall, slim, weather-beaten, and shy. They stared at each other in
silence. The serenity was broken, however, by a Jordanian policeman who started firing questions at me: 'What are you doing on
this wall? Do you intend to stay long? What country are you
from? What town? What is your profession? What is the reason
for your visit?' My few words of Arabic seemed to placate him,
but the spell was broken. A group of Arabs sat in the sun,
weighted down by inactivity. *'Marhaba – Marsalaam!*

By four o'clock, the Via Dolorosa was deserted and overlaid
with shadows. Women do not sit in cafés, still less alone, and my
neighbour's disapproval bordered on contempt. Unbuttoned and
collarless, with a filthy black beret and a barbarous beard, he
puffed ever more noisily at a hubble-bubble. I was relieved to
be rescued by Father D. and Father S., Dominican priests with a
sense of humour quite equal to their humanity and culture. One
habitually wore an Australian bush-hat and was more pro-Jewish
than Ben Gurion. The other was inclined to sympathize with the
Arabs. 'You and your Jews,' he would say affectionately to his
friends who would lead his pilgrim-tourists in a fervent 'Our
Father' at Yad-Vachem, the black marble sanctuary dedicated to
Jewish victims of Nazi persecution.

The streets are never quiet for long here, and soon there were
Orthodox priests with black beards and tubular head-dresses,
American girls with maxi-thighs and mini-skirts, hippies show-

ing their navels or sweating in embroidered goatskin gear, tourists and more tourists, and Israeli soldiers walking with a child or a girl-friend. A young man and two Jewish girls in trousers greeted a young Arab sitting near me.

Suddenly it seemed that the tourists gave way to the Orthodox Jews on their way to the Wailing Wall to offer prayers at the beginning of the Sabbath. They came hurrying in compact groups from Mea-Shearim where they worked and traded in workshops and salesrooms aglitter with seven-branched candelabra, ceremonial skull-caps of embroidered satin, *tallithim* or large white prayer-shawls. They were Hassidim members of the strictest, most devout of Jewish sects. The men wore frock-coats and black hats or, since today was a feast day, frock-coats of brocaded satin, and huge, flat hats of brown fur called *shtremmels*. The men, young or old, had long ringlets one on each side of the face. The younger men had unbuttoned their frock-coats, and the skirts flapped in time with their steps. They looked just like crows with their offspring held by the wingtip, sweet offspring in long shorts and short trousers, all unimpeachably black, with round hats pushed back, framing their fresh, cheery faces. Many were fair, and a few had red hair. One splendid man had a deep russet beard, and with his frock-coat and fur hat one could imagine him to be an Amsterdam diamond-merchant painted by Rembrandt.

An opulent trio in satin frock-coats flapped past me. One looked like Dirk Bogarde, the second like Christ, and the third like Gregory Peck. Alas, they were the exception. Most of them had the wan look of lettuces grown under glass; their eyes were fixed on the distant hills of Judea. They had round shoulders and sagging paunches. They were, no doubt, the pride and joy of their ladies whose heads were shaven as the Law demands but whose faces were sometimes softened by fringes of false hair just visible under their turban. They were not much to look at though one was about twenty, with a jade-green suit the colour of her eyes, and a skirt showing a daring glimpse of knee. Her pudding-face of a husband looked sulky and put-out.

I joined the current sweeping towards the Wall. The street sloped gently up-hill, shrinking in the shade of the high arched walls, past a delightful stone fountain. There was a smell of urine and refuse. Lively, grinning Arab children skipped and shouted, 'Wailing Wall! Wailing Wall!' The crowd veered left, up a dozen steps into a dark alley like the tube at rush hour. I could see only the broad black back of the Hassid ahead. The pressure eased, and we were in a vast square where a Jewish soldier searched my handbag. A grenade had exploded the week before, wounding eight people. At the far side of the square stood the Wailing Wall of tall stones, all that remained of the temple Herod built on the ruins of Solomon's temple.

A chain hangs between two slender iron pillars, and only the men are allowed through, one by one. Their heads covered with small black caps, they take prayer books and, facing the Wall, they intone their prayers, punctuating them with shuffling. It was like a sea moving in rhythm with the chant, swelling and behind them others came and went: fathers with their small sons, overawed tourists, soldiers, civilians, local residents, visitors from abroad, each here in devotion, but devotion nothing like that of conventional church attendances. Here was an electric, emotional excitement. The Jews had only had access to the Wall since the Six-Day War. Before that it was just one side of a narrow street which the Jordanians used as a rubbish-dump. Now, the Jews had razed the hideous slum behind the narrow street and opened up this uncluttered approach to the Wall, where it stands out clearly as a monument restored to the full dignity of a sanctuary.

Edging my way along the chain between the spectators and worshippers, I reached the third of the Wall reserved for women. The shorn, turbaned ladies were performing the same shuffle as they prayed, but their movements were more restrained. I stepped forward, declining one of the Hebrew prayer books, but obeying a firm finger pointing at the collection box. I earned a smile.

Now I was able to see the Wall at close range. I am not a particularly reverent person by nature, but it stirred me. Its rich

golden stones are covered with little holes, like old skin long-
exposed to the sun; small rolls of paper are tucked in the crevices,
and they spell out countless prayers and petitions. I touched the
old thing; it was cool and smooth.

A few yards farther on, a barrier seals off the dig which was
begun to uncover the foundations of Solomon's earlier temple.
The success of the enterprise was assured, and two stones from
the great temple were already lying in the earth far below.

It is possible to love Jerusalem like a person, delicately and
excitedly, passionately. One is then spellbound, touched, fatigued,
thrilled, tired, beguiled, offended, and love is willingly given.
It is love with its drawbacks, its impulses, its anxious hearts and
its extended hands.

Out of the fragrant hotel gardens, I went in the pink cool of
morning and up the Nablus Road, leaving the beautiful roofless
Turkish house behind and passing the Safiehs' closed town-
travel agency and the unattended handicraft shops selling Palestinian dresses, Hebron glassware and even seven-branched cande-
labras. The shopkeepers in this Christian-Arab no-man's-land
spent their time gossiping among the few battered houses, whose
gardens still smell sweet but whose shutters were pulled to
and whose owners had fled to Amman or Lausanne.

I made my way to St Stephen's basilica, which is also a bible
school and archaeological institute. I had a letter to Father de
Vaux, the 'discoverer' of the Dead Sea Scrolls. He died a few
months later, but he was then the pre-eminent Palestinian archaeologist. I waited for him in an icy parlour.

He was, when he at last arrived, such a formidable figure that
he might have stepped from a portrait by Philippe de Cham-
paigne. Nothing about him put me at ease – not his great height,
nor his grey eyes, nor his sturdy straight nose and full mouth
framed by the grey beard. His long, muscular hands lay spread
on the white robe and he expressed himself with devastating
precision. He showed scant charity as he waited for my ques-

tions, contriving, this haughty Christian, to make me feel as if I had bothered Zeus himself at his labours.

I asked if the presence of the Israeli military forces interfered with archaeological pursuits and I felt that he, like most of the other Dominicans from Palestine, was an Arab sympathizer. The Jews had evicted him and taken over the excavation sites. Some Israeli archaeologists, he admitted, were first-class, like Ygal Yadin, whom he admired though he did not approve of his politics. 'As he very well knows,' he added. 'The trouble is that, having good archaeologists of their own, they don't need foreigners.' They were making large-scale excavations all over the country, partly out of scientific interest and partly to establish links between their present and their past. He stressed the contrast between historical insignificance and material poverty and the immense spiritual influence which Palestine had exerted. The poverty accounted for the lack of substantial works of art, in sharp contrast to the marvels found by André Parrot at Mari and by Leonard Woolley at Ur. 'Culture,' he said, 'can be likened to a pyramid, and the width of its base is dependent on a country's material prosperity.'

He returned majestically to his private work, leaving me to find my own way out of the ark, confusing corridors, where I found the mischievous blue eyes of Father Avril, who was to take me and two friends to Jericho.

We left on the old road winding through the hills above the furrowed desert. On the far side of a wide, deep gorge, the blue bulb-shaped domes of a Greek Orthodox monastery, surrounded by a bed of green, perched above the gorge as these monasteries have done for fifteen centuries. To our right a tiny white mosque stood like a speck in an expanse of crushed stone. It was known as the Pope's mosque, for when Paul VI visited the Holy Land in 1964, Jordan gave him the land to build a hospital for the deaf and dumb, and the Arabs were so furious that they erected this mosque during the night, rendering the site inviolable.

Nearer to Jericho, Father Avril's grey goatee bristled at King Isham's palace, handsome, ornate, its windows shaded by zigzags of stone, noble ancestors of Le Corbusier's *brise-soleils,* and (oddly) several statues of buxom women, doubtless reflecting the King's sexual appetites in what was, after all, a folly.

Jericho was quiet and still in the siesta hour, though most of the little houses among the bougainvilleas appeared deserted, their paintwork peeling, the inhabitants fled. The roads were sweetened by the scent of an orange grove. The town was a fertile oasis which from the desert looked like a rich spread of green velvet.

From Jericho a flat, lifeless arid plain called the Ghor stretches to the edge of the Dead Sea. The Dead Sea is like blue treacle, with so much salt that one can float erect in it. There is a large, seedy hotel by the shore, and across the water are the Moab heights, changing slowly from pink to violet. A series of reports and some small puffs of smoke marked the Jordanian artillery having a go at the kibbutzim close by the border.

We drove along the Dead Sea to Khirbet Qumran in a chaotic landscape of sharp cliffs. In the seventh century B.C. Qumran was the home of the Essenes, a Manichaean tribe who held aloof from other Jewish people whom they regarded as amoral and materialistic. They were like Jewish Jansenites, thinking solely in terms of good and evil, light and dark. John the Baptist lived among them before he left to preach Christian tolerance on the shores of the Dead Sea. It is probable that Christ too spent time with the Essenes.

Father Avril painted a grim picture of these austere, pious people who spent their time studying and annotating the Scriptures: unshakeable bastions of religious and intellectual orthodoxy whose severe standards were reflected in so many other sects. It was all very remote from the spirit of Voltaire.

Qumran is the place where a shepherd found fragments of ancient parchment and where in 1952 Father de Vaux started scouring the area for the Dead Sea Scrolls.

The Dead Sea was turning evening-pink, and clouds collected

on the Moab heights. We pushed on north towards the Allenby Bridge, where most of the goods flow between East and West-Bank Jordan. The desert sprawled between cliffs and ravines, and the road ran through abandoned villages; Bedouins squatted by their black tents, and the cliffs were full of caves giving natural shelter to the guerrillas. A tall, sun-tanned, fair-haired soldier stood in front of the car, his legs astride and his sub-machine-gun ready. He told us we couldn't go any farther; he obviously meant what he said, and our arguments, our jokes, and even my eyelashes were of no avail. We returned as the road began to darken purple. Soldiers urged us to hurry. I remembered being told in Finks that the roads in the occupied territories were unsafe at night. But the car was running smoothly, the air was cool and my cigarette tasted as cigarettes should. It seemed less perilous than an evening drive along the Boulevard Saint-Michel during a student demonstration.

The floodlit walls of Jerusalem surged out of the dark night as we approached the Jaffa Gate.

We travelled north of Jerusalem into Judea, through the Arab town of Ramallah (where the shops were open in defiance of a strike called by Al Fatah), and on towards Nablus, where a grenade had caused two Israeli casualties the day before.

Four childlike helmeted faces guarded the road where it entered the town. There seemed to be no other troops, though Nablus, capital of Samaria, was known for the irascibility of its fifty thousand inhabitants, always in fiery opposition to authority from the Old Testament kings to Hussein, whom they held in great contempt. Under Israeli rule they were as defiant and uncooperative as ever. The mayor was well known as an independent character hostile to the occupying forces who, to their credit, had never tried to replace him with a more tractable figure. The strike-call was more successful here than in Ramallah, and all the shops in the main street were closed. The curfew was to begin at 4 p.m. The atmosphere was certainly not calm or relaxed, and the streets were deserted. We tried to enter the Old Town of fine houses dating from the Turkish occupation, but we were stopped by an Israeli police officer, who spoke to us in Arabic.

At lunch, I joined my Dominican friends, Father D. and Father S. who invited me to tag along with their excursion party of stolid, god-fearing French, past their prime and blissfully unaware of the 'complications' of the country.

'Is this place really under foreign occupation?'

'Why, yes!'

'Who is in control, then? The Arabs?'

'No, no. The Jews.'

'So we aren't in Israel?'

'It used to be Jordan. It still is, in theory.'

'But no one has asked us for our passports!'

Jewish policemen talking Arabic, Israeli Arabs talking Hebrew, cabinet ministers washing dishes in kibbutzim, Iraqi battalions previously stationed in Jordan. All this was a trifle confusing.

'And this Al Fatah we keep hearing about: where is it?'

I pointed at the barman. Everyone within earshot roared with laughter.

Joseph, one of the taxi-drivers attached to the party, recognized me from a previous visit and agreed to take us through the Old Town while the pilgrims ate their dessert and tried to catch up on current affairs. Joseph was a pleasant, sturdy young man, married with a child. He sometimes regretted being married. If he had been single he would have emigrated to America. He saw no future for young Palestinians, as the Arab travel-agencies were unable to compete with the Jewish ones and now had very few customers.

We threaded through the Old Town, and coffee-drinkers in a café doorway called to Joseph, gaping at us in disbelief. There were no tourists here. The most progressive members of the bourgeoisie, plump women in European dress, calculated the length of my skirt. The markets were colourful and cool and the traders were friendly, obviously satisfied that I was with Joseph. I could tell, though, that many of them thought I was an Israeli, and their faces hardened. Joseph got embarrassed and annoyed. 'Françaoui! French!' he explained. 'We're all Jews in somebody's eyes,' I said smiling, and he stared at me perplexed.

'Please, madame,' he said, 'tell your readers that peace must return to this country. The war has brought misery to both sides. The Jews are good people. We can live with them. We can, believe me, even if many Arabs tell you the opposite. I know them.'

*Au revoir,* Joseph. Peace be with you and with all men of goodwill. *Salam Alekum.*

Samaria has aroused the covetousness of foreign rulers through-out the ages. In the eighth century B.C., King Sargon of Assyria deported thirty thousand of its nomadic inhabitants to Mesopotamia and put in their place tough, boorish settlers from Babylon. Meso-Samaritans returned from exile worshipping heathen gods, like the Babylonian intruders. And the faithful Jews who had remained in Samaria would deal with neither group and decreed them unfit to rebuild the Temple, which there-fore remained unbuilt until the fifth century B.C. The stout city wall raided by the Jewish King Omri still stands in Sebastye, the ancient capital of Samaria. The wall backs on to a Roman theatre on the side of the hill which King Omri bought from Shemer, to whom Samaria owes its name. These kings were merely chieftains of nomadic tribes with realms little more than a few hills.

Another stop among the buttercups and poppies of Samaria is the old Canaanite city of Sechem, whose slender columns, like those of Sakkarah in Egypt, date from the beginning of the Middle Bronze Age, some eighteen hundred years before Christ. Even when they were built, Sechem was a thousand years old. Abraham arrived with his cattle and offspring, about seventeen hundred B.C., and two hundred years later his descendant Jacob raised an altar to El, God of Israel.

Until the Six-Day War, a small impoverished community of these unruly Samaritans lived on the West Bank. Ben Gurion supplied them with subsidies through a Palestinian Dominican,

Father Sarkis, another of the delightful ironies of the Middle East where disparate pieces suddenly interlock like a giant jigsaw. The Israeli government was just resettling the community in Gezarim, where ugly concrete houses had been built for them, where the roofs bristled with machine-guns and Israeli soldiers watched the big green valley below the village. It is the only village in the world where the paschal lamb is still sacrificed.

In a gentle morning breeze the kibbutz at Hazorea was surrounded by vineyards and orange groves. Mr Bierger took me to lunch: he was a tall, stooping man of fifty-two with a thin, lined face and brooding brown eyes; a native of Breslau, he had been through many wild adventures while buying arms for the Jews before the 1948 war.

Everyone on the kibbutz got a personal allowance of three hundred Israeli pounds a year, about thirty pounds sterling. It ran a library and was one of the older and wealthier kibbutzim. Founded in the thirties by German philosophers and doctors who came to dig at the gravelly soil, it retains a strong intellectual tradition. Each member has a bicycle, and, as the cars belong to the community, they can be borrowed readily. Clothing comes from a co-operative, and any outside income is handed over, without exception, to the community's financial director. A newcomer spends a trial year and then the entire community votes on his admittance, the theory being that one man can make a mistake but not three hundred. There are no bosses or boards of directors; everything is decided by ballot.

The surrounding hills were covered with the pine-forests planted in memory of the victims of the concentration camps, a more expressive memorial than so many of the ghastly monuments of Europe.

There were fragments of Roman pillars emerging from the flower-beds, and the museum, which had sliding panels opening on an interior courtyard and was oddly reminiscent of Japan, was full of statues, pottery, coins and glassware from Neolithic, Roman, Byzantine and Islamic periods, all found beneath the surface of this Edenic soil. The first pioneers found a rocky plain infested with insects and scorpions, and lashed by winds that drove the yellow dust into their faces. They knew nothing about agriculture, but studied textbooks to produce crops and cattle which stand any comparison. The cows of Hazorea, I was assured, gave more milk than Flemish Friesians, and the corn-fields yielded more than those in France. Hazorea had even had demonstrations arising from the problems of its surplus produce.

The lathes were turning in the furniture factory, strewn with chips and shavings, where Scandinavian tables and chairs were being assembled, varnished and stacked ready for dispatch. The plastics factory roared like a squadron of tanks, and long metal rollers produced sheets of synthetic material. Bierger admitted that this was his brainchild, and he was especially proud of a laboratory where technicians greeted him with obvious warmth. But the zeal was not everywhere, and in a corner of the factory a bearded Englishman and a local worker were reading comic books while their roller malfunctioned. We had almost to clamber over a group of scruffy, dishevelled young men who didn't move and stared after us without a smile or acknowledgement. After this, I began to find poor Bierger's disillusion easier to understand.

The dusty shelves of the library were stacked with books in English, French and Hebrew. Many were stained and falling apart, a slightly distressing sight to someone who tends to revere books.

An elegant lady in grey slacks passed us, with delicate features and a hair-style which made her seem oddly out of place so far from the eighteenth green of the Saint-Cloud golf club. I wondered about her history and the events which brought her to Hazora. So many of these people had extraordinary stories of death, upheaval, courage and determination.

The dairy had two hundred cows. A red-haired giant of a man with a thick neck and powerful hands was tending them. He looked like a typical German peasant. The cows' udders swelled to the strains of Rodrigo's *Concerto de Aranjuez,* and they drank discoloured water from a large concrete tank. Bierger surveyed the beaten earth and reeking straw, in wonder at the long years of dedication and self-sacrifice which had gone into this cherished victory over the Friesians. Milk is hardly my favourite drink, even skimmed, strained, pasteurized and chilled, but Bierger handed me a huge glass of fresh, warm, dull-coloured milk, and I put on an act worthy of the Queen of England sampling cobra-venom on a visit to a remote tribe in Bechuanaland.

As I drove away from this world which was no longer Bierger's, his tall, stooping figure receded and disappeared behind the trees which he had planted to outlive him.

We were invited north to Tiberiades to visit the Old Lion, Ben Gurion.

And then suddenly, as we raced across an open plain, two steel flashes came from east to west across the sky. From their triangular shape, I thought they were Mirages, but we got out of the car, 'just in case', prepared to throw ourselves flat. The aircrafts bore down on the centre of the plain, dived vertically very low and strafed a target no more than two hundred yards from a Jewish farmer, who scarcely lifted his head. The planes climbed back into the sky, completing their tight manoeuvre.

Through valley after valley we arrived at the town of Tiberias, trim, modern and fast-expanding, where any of the friendly people would have hopped into the car and shown us the way to the Tiberiades Kinnereth Hotel. Ben Gurion was striding away with a bodyguard in hot pursuit. It was part of a daily five-mile routine at the pace of a light-infantryman, and we ordered orangeade and waited for him.

A dark pretty girl and a young man checked us quickly and carefully, and ushered us into a large room looking on the lake. A narrow divan was set against the left-hand wall, and a work-table was laden with books and files. Ben Gurion was silhouetted against the light, and rose to greet us, wearing a dark, well-cut three-piece suit. He was short and hefty, with a large head set in broad shoulders; wings of white hair sprang from his forehead. We told him a little about ourselves and he listened attentively, taking stock of us. His complexion was golden and his lips pale. His blue-grey eyes would wrinkle into a smile, or just as suddenly dart a look of steely determination. His mouth was firm, sensitive and animated, falling slightly at the corners, the mouth of a man used to controlling his own feelings and the lives of others. He leaned back in his chair, clutching the lapels of his jacket with small, sturdy, dark-flecked hands.

He talked about his childhood in Russia, and his grandfather who perched him on his knees as a boy of four and taught him Hebrew. Ben Gurion's English was fast and fluent, but with a heavy accent which made some of his remarks difficult to follow. In 1890 neighbouring Jews would gather in his father's house to talk of Palestine. At the age of eleven he founded a Zionist association among his schoolmates, who received a copeck each for their loyalty.

At twenty-one, in 1905, he arrived in Jaffa and walked to Jerusalem. It took him a day and a half with a knapsack on his back. A Jewish girl showed him around the old city and he never opened his lips. Later the same girl married Ben Zvi who became the first vice-president of the state of Israel. 'I was very shy in those days,' Ben Gurion explained with a smile. 'The two things that made the biggest impression on me in Jerusalem were the Wailing Wall and the fact that the Jews living in the city spoke over a dozen different languages. My immediate reaction was that they must quickly learn to adopt a single language, and I was convinced from the outset that it ought to be Hebrew.'

Obsessed with his visions of the future, he seemed unresponsive to buildings and landscapes. He moved from topic to topic, explaining the background with great courtesy. Realizing that we already knew a few things about Palestine, he slapped the table with his little hand and beamed at us. His lower lip swelled with pleasure and merriment and he paused only to search for a name or date.

He talked then of his battles with Lord Lloyd, pronouncing the name so that it sounded like 'Lloyt'. The latter had been strongly opposed to Zionism but agreed to let Ben Gurion call on him in

London and persuade him. Ben Gurion strode about the room, mimicking Lord 'Lloyt's' style, and sat down again, taking a fresh grip on his lapels.

More determinedly he talked about 1948, the immense risks involved, and his fight to free Jerusalem from the Arab stranglehold.

He appeared to be a man of iron, endowed with such indomitable moral fibre that nothing could deflect him from his chosen course: and yet he was full of humanity, captivating, not with the accomplishment of a guest holding forth at dinner but with a deep magnetism which fires emotion, lifting people to new heights. I thought of his wife Paula who died in 1967 and who hovered over him, not hesitating to interrupt a cabinet meeting or a distinguished visitor with her gruff, 'Your milk, David.'

Moshe Sharett told him in 1948 that the British High Commissioner considered it sheer folly to defend Jerusalem. He replied simply, 'So do I.' But he instructed Sharett to inform the War Cabinet only of the High Commissioner's opinion, not his own.

After an hour and a half the young man returned and told us curtly that the interview was over. But Ben Gurion was thoroughly enjoying himself, and his recollections, laced with humour, grew richer and richer, while his memory for facts and figures never faltered. He talked about Lord Moyne's plan to evacuate part of Germany in 1945 and to use it as a resettlement area for Jews from the concentration camps. Ben Gurion had scoffed at the idea. 'It took machine-guns to get them out of Germany,' he reminded Lord Moyne, 'and it will take a good deal more than machine-guns to get them to go back.' The word 'machine-gun' eluded him for a moment, 'I'm forgetting all the words I ever knew,' he grumbled.

It grew dark at seven and he talked on in the shadowy room.

'Modiano?' he said to me. 'Why, that's an old Sephardic name,' and he talked of Salonika, which until 1940 had been mainly Sephardic. He had gone there to learn Turkish in the days of the Ottoman Empire. He doubled up with laughter as he recalled how the Sephardim, who imagined themselves so superior looked down on the Ashkenazes as pimps because one of them, a native of Poland, had dared to open a brothel in that god-fearing town of Salonika. Ben Gurion remembered the language problems he had with his landlady. He would speak Russian, which a friend would render into Turkish for another friend, who translated the Turkish phrases into Ladino, the curious fifteenth-century Spanish-Arabic language of the Sephardim.

We parted on the warmest terms with an invitation to visit him at Sde Boker, his kibbutz in the Negev. The young usher looked disapproving, but I hopped gaily along the corridor.

The high-relief lions on St Stephen's gate were picked out gold in the rising sun, and I walked by the ramparts looking down into the Cedron valley, loving the tawny-coloured hills touched pink by the soft light. Father Blondel, another plump, red-faced, cheerful Dominican, was to show me St Anne's Chapel, one of the many Frankish crusader churches of the twelfth century. All have the simplicity of romanesque architecture, massive, elegant and affecting. St Anne's was hit by a shell in 1967 and part of the roof was destroyed. The French government rejected the Israeli offer to pay for the damage.

A ray of sunlight struck across the square, silent nave. A plaque commemorated M. Neuville, the French Consul-general who died in Jerusalem in 1952. Like Botta in nineteenth-century Iraq, Neuville was a hard-working consul, an imaginative archaeologist and an eminent Arabist. During the siege of Jerusalem he was barricaded with his family and colleagues in the consulate close by the King David Hotel. At one point there were violent thumps on the door and two members of the Haganah presented the orderly with a cardboard box. 'With General Shaltiel's compliments.' The colourful, legendary general, exploring the cellars of one of the city's hotels, had chanced upon a cache of Camembert cheese and champagne which he thought no one would appreciate so much as his friend Neuville.

Father Blondel had been standing in the doorway of St Stephen's in 1948, just after the Jews captured the city, when Levy-Eskol greeted him, holding out his hand. He took it, telling him that the monastery was full of starving Arab refugees whom the Jewish army had ordered them to look after during the fighting. Levy-Eskol, a gentle, understanding man, sent a lorry-load of supplies. But Father Blondel was much taken to task by his religious superiors and fellow-priests, not so much because they were pro-Arab as because they were anti-Jewish.

Had the Jewish soldiers kicked the door of St Stephen's as the Consul general had told me? Father Blondel assured me that this was not so and that they behaved in a highly disciplined manner.

'And at Our Lady of Sion?' I cast myself somewhat mischievously in the role of devil's advocate, remembering the quip of my Samarian guide. 'Throughout the centuries it was the mission of the Ladies of Sion to convert the Jews. Today there is reason to fear that it is the Jews who are converting the Ladies of Sion.'

I seemed to wander about Jerusalem day and night. I wondered if I would wear my legs out or drown myself with coffee.

Past the Haram again, and the Armenian church whose icons and glazed tiles brought the entire Old Testament to life with disarming simplicity, and into the old Jewish quarter. The Jews had lived here for ever; before the first Aliyah there were thirty thousand of them and successive travellers, from Nahmanides in the thirteenth century to Sir Moses Montefiore in the nineteenth, have talked of this quarter as a place of squalor and disease, never free of plague. How little it appealed to illustrious western visitors like Lamartine, Chateaubriand and Loti, who were utterly horrified by what for others is the ineffable beauty of Jerusalem!

The Jordanians evicted the Jews at the start of the War of Independence, and it is still the home of the poorest Arabs, with rubbish rotting in the mud under the gloomy vaults; dishevelled, rather fetching children shouting 'Baksheesh! Baksheesh!' and the sound of yelps, smacks, and shrieking kids.

Narrow staircases led off narrow passages into lightless build-

A Hassidim Jew praying
in front of the Wailing
Wall, wearing his
*shtremmel*, fur hat, and
*tallith*, his white
prayer-shawl

A party of Kibbutzniks
coming out from a guided
visit to the Holy
Sepulchre

At Masada, the author on the site of the synagogue of the Zealots

The Dead Sea and Sodom, seen from a crack in the great tooth-like rock of
Masada, rising from the valley

ings, the whole scene smelling of urine. A boy of fifteen made a grab at me. 'Where you go?' he asked aggressively, and three others appeared from nowhere, pressing round me. They held on to me menacingly. 'Yalla, yalla!' 'Get away from me!' Fortunately I alarmed them enough and they fled in panic.

It was a relief after that grim maze to find the friendly bustle of the market-place, where you could buy everything, fresh fruit, old clothes, brass trinkets, and shimmering fabric. A young nun hurried past with a large aluminium stew-pan. She had her sleeves sensibly rolled up and smiled broadly at me as she bustled by. Orthodox Jews were making for the Wall, curl-papers fluttering in the breeze. An aged Arab in a filthy turban, blocking the way, whacked at a donkey whose small stubborn hooves refused to advance. Bedouins swathed in black stared at me with coal-black eyes; others stared too, young men in white shirts and dark trousers, knee-high, and children yelping, 'Damascus Gate! Damascus Gate!' Palestinian girls roved in small groups, all mini-skirts and short, plump thighs. There were tall, trousered German women, and their close-cropped husbands; American women in pink and orange, hen-pecking; and the French, the élite tourists of the moment, debating, discussing, commenting as if no one else could possibly understand them. As the arches intersect and the walls and streets curve around each other, the races and nationalities and religions come together and part, timelessly, intoxicatingly, exhaustingly, fascinatingly.

The Christian-Arab quarter is lighter, the streets broader and the shops bigger. Ladies' outfitters become neon paradises of fluffy nylon night-gowns and vast satin dresses. The men and boys were dressed in the European style, but in a sudden patch of darkness by a wall a peasant woman squatted beside a basket of vegetables. Carters and donkey-drivers cleared a way with guttural 'Halloos!' Amongst all the commotion was a sense of space and calm. The fat, friendly Mr Barakat's shop was overflowing with splendours and delights, and his slim young son greeted me in sprightly French. Sipping coffee in the cool, sandalwood-smelling shop, I chose copper teapots and knick-knacks. I showed no signs of haggling, and the son, with a nod from his father, reduced the prices, throwing in a few small presents. We parted well-content with each other.

With half an hour before lunch, I hurried back through the markets to the Wailing Wall. It was Passover, and joy and emotion shone from every face in the shuffling, praying lines.

A stout French lady concluded to her companions in a piercing voice, 'Ah well, they might as well pray. Our Lord and Our Lady were Jews, after all!'

The big ochre consulate blazes with bougainvilleas, but the garden is prim with rose-trees at two-foot intervals, oddly un-exuberant for such a setting. In the eighteenth-century drawing-room the Consul left me with S.M., the official in charge of cultural affairs at the Quai d'Orsay. Then a nice-looking, overawed couple arrived. He was headmaster of the French School, and his wife, in her Sunday best, bubbled with excitement to be lunching with the Consul general. They spoke fluent French with an oriental accent; and the Consul's man-ner was, as ever, slightly distant, as if his thoughts were else-where. The 'Quai' has never bred much human warmth. S.M. was worse, listening without looking at them and not wait-ing to launch into a flow of quite irrelevant rhetoric, assuring me, in an aside, that it was good for 'these people' to learn French. French he considered imperative for international exchanges not technical exchanges, of course, but cultural ex-changes at the international level. That was all right by me, but I couldn't help remarking that a young Israeli would waste a lot of time, reading for a degree in French, when he would be living in a nation which speaks Hebrew, Arabic and English.

The two gothic towers of the Holy Sepulchre were criss-crossed with scaffolding. Jordanian police and an Israeli soldier chatted on guard by the main door. Inside, an elegant blonde European knelt to kiss the great slab of purple marble on the spot where Christ's body was anointed. Snatches of a Gregorian chant came from deep inside, and a line of brown-frocked

Franciscans holding candles came two by two, singing psalms, from the small side-chapels whose vaults were covered with fine mosaic scenes of the Old Testament on a gold background. Upstairs and down and then retracing my way, almost lost in dark corners among mosaics and far too much gilt, I sat down to rest on a stone bench. A threadbare little man sat beside me singing the praises of the *Guide Bleu* over my shoulder. He was a Nusseibeh and showed me a cutting from the *Jerusalem Post* recalling that the Nusseibehs were made custodians of the Holy Sepulchre in 1333, a privilege to be handed down from father to son. A Moslem family was chosen when the Christians were divided and weakened after the fall of the Frankish kingdom of Jerusalem. It is much the same today, and responsibility for the Holy Sepulchre is shared by Franciscans, Armenians and the Greek Orthodox Church. Their rivalries are legendary, and the Greeks are said to have been kept waiting for, on one occasion, two hours while the Armenians droned on and on at the altar for no purpose other than to delay the Orthodox Mass. Father Couasnon, a Dominican charged with the restoration work, to the chagrin of the Franciscans, told me of his difficulties with the Armenians who, with limitless wealth thanks to the Gulbenkian bequest, wanted to plaster everything with gold, and bridled at the mention of bare stones or plain arches. Nor were the Armenians the only troublemakers: if one of them were to dust a single step on a staircase in the Greek area, civil war broke out. Before the Six-Day War the Jordanian police would stand by to intervene in these affrays.

A party of Israeli boys in traditional little black skull-caps was too much for the old Nusseibeh.

'They monopolize everything,' he moaned. 'All the guides are Jewish. There is now an examination, and they turned me down. Still, they are not here for ever. Al Fatah are very strong and yesterday they blew up all the telephone lines.'

Over these trivialities runs the timeless variety of people: bearded Greek Orthodox priests; tall, stately Russians in black, with long white hair pinned back into a flat bun; Italian nuns gliding like swans; brown-robed Franciscans; kibbutzniks in jean and short-sleeved shirts and cotton hats; an Ethiopian, black as night; lordly Arabs in flowing chestnut and white *keffiehs;* and the elegant blonde who had kissed the marble, now escorted by a neat and proper Frenchman. This was a most richly flavoured spectacle, with a telephone by the door in direct contact with the police station.

For the Israeli reunification of Jerusalem was not recognized by the Powers which stood by the 1947 United Nations partition plan, and these Powers had insisted on maintaining their consulates in both parts of the city. The decision challenged the city council's authority, and in July 1969 the Consuls General had declined the invitation to an exhibition of Armenian treasures in the Jordanian part of the city, on the grounds that Teddy Kolek, the Israeli mayor, would be officiating at the opening ceremony. Mr Kolek retaliated by depriving the consular offices in the Arab quarter of diplomatic privileges. Rate demands were sent out with the threat that unless payment was prompt the consuls' belongings would be distrained. This loggerhead situation was solved only when the French Consul general, urged his American, British, Italian and Belgian colleagues to write to the Mayor that, conforming to *corpus separatum,* their consulates in the respective parts of the city constituted a single administrative entity. This was interpreted by the Council to mean the end of dual consulates and a *de facto* recognition of the 'reunification of the city under the authority of the Israeli city council'. The consuls, however, insisted that a real change had taken place, as they had never recognized the partitioning of Jerusalem in the first place. As a result of these exchanges, consular staffs in the Old City need not fear a visit from the bailiff.

I went into dinner with my good friend Piero Founi, a Palestinian journalist, and another man who ran a bookshop. They were talking about censorship, and though they agreed that the freedom of the press had increased, although they were not allowed to describe guerrillas as 'resistance groups', they felt that they were not given all the information offered to Western reporters.

I quoted Ygal Allon, 'They are free to say and write whatever they like, just so long as they don't shoot at us.'

As the chairs scraped around our hostess's table, the journalist likened the situation to the Nazi Occupation, much to the consternation of the French guests. 'Just you wait and keep your eyes open,' he warned. 'You haven't seen anything yet! "They" don't take hostages,' he went on, 'but "they" round up people in the streets and throw them in prison and torture them; there are over ten thousand rotting in Israeli jails.'

The consul's wife looked as if her roast were spoiling, and Founi changed the subject, asking why Arab communiqués were either exaggerated or false. 'We do lie and we are perfectly right to do so. People believe the communiqués and are carried away to support Al Fatah. *C'est la guerre*. We *must* lie!'

A French monk named Father Gélin, exasperated by the same point, once said to me that it was not a question of lying but of eloquence. Nasser describes in his book, *Philosophy of Revolution,* how at the height of the 1948 War he heard Cairo Radio assuring Egyptians that his battalion was sprinting to victory across Sinai, while it was really in full retreat, desperately short of food and ammunition. He smashed the small transistor, swearing that if ever he held power he would never lie to the people. Perhaps one's word east of Montpellier loses its contractual value, becoming subtle politeness and courtesy, a means of captivating an audience, capturing them, even. At its best this becomes an art, but otherwise it is the spouting of tired, empty words and phrases.

The journalist's eyes were bulging with the successes of Al Fatah. The Jews were so terrified of bombs that they would not get into their cars without checking under the chassis. But the situation called for thousands of bombs, millions. The Jews would have to go. Surely we French were not opposed to the idea of a resistance movement? With or without a resistance movement, the day would come when there would be no such thing as the State of Israel.

This silenced the French but not the bookseller, who averred that the State of Israel was already defunct. 'No, it isn't!' bellowed the journalist. 'It's very much alive!' There were a hundred million Arabs whose pride would not accept a settlement. The Jews must be driven out. The next war might be lost, but after that they would win with atom bombs from the Russians who were the only people benefiting from the situation. Egypt lost by it, Hussein lost by it, the Arabs lost by it, and Israel and Arafat needn't even be mentioned. Meanwhile, neither the journalist nor the bookseller would go into West Jerusalem for fear of being bundled into cars and beaten up in broad daylight. Even Founi, a veteran in such matters, was utterly bewildered by such sweeping untruths.

Could such fears be justified? Such incidents can occur anywhere except perhaps in England. Did the forces of Occupation pursue a systematic policy of brutality and torture? That was the real question, and where did law and order become repression?

'Being an occupied power is only worse than being an occupying one.'

The Arabs of West-Bank Jordan were the occupied now, seething with humiliation and anger and yet unresponsive to the redemptive rattle of the guerrillas' machine-guns. The wild predictions of Nayef Hawatnieh, head of the P.D.F.L.P.*, that the West-Bank Jordan would become a second Vietnam, had come to nothing. The hills of Judea and Samaria gave nothing like the cover of the Vietnamese jungle. The 'resistance movement' should have operated as the Vietcong did in the occupied areas 'like fish in water'. But the urban Palestinians, mostly merchants and members of the liberal professions, were not at all eager to accommodate such fish. Those who sheltered guerrillas were likely to see their homes blown up by the Israeli army, and those who refused to shelter them could also lose their lives like the

* Popular Democratic Front for the Liberation of Palestine, a body composed of between four and five thousand men.

five members of a single family killed for 'collaborating with the enemy' in 1969.

In spite of this, nearly eight thousand 'resident Arabs'* exercised their right to vote in Jerusalem municipal elections in October 1969. Teddy Kollek was characteristically quick to interpret their participation as 'recognition of Israel authority over the city', and indeed his personal prestige and record of achievements may have been the prime cause of this unexpected development. The old hatred endured, and though Hussein stamped out Al Fatah in Jordan the Arabs still complained of the 'hardness' and 'cruelty' of Israeli occupation. They resented the destruction of Arab homes in reprisal for local incidents, a measure which also earned for Dayan criticism from certain Israeli members of parliament and the Jewish public, though he argued that it was a necessity and that 'people who risked seeing their homes destroyed would think twice before harbouring terrorists'. He stated that five hundred and sixteen Arab houses had been destroyed in this way in the period between the Six-Day War and the end of 1969, and that it was the British, in 1945, who first resorted to such measures. Although Dayan claimed not to favour collective punishment, he made the point that in the same thirty months Al Fatah had killed a hundred and fourteen Israelis, including thirty-seven civilians, and injured six hundred and thirty-four, of whom three hundred and forty-seven were civilians.

The Arabs, predictably, level charges of torture which the Israelis predictably reject. An Israeli general with the Army of Occupation firmly and convincingly denied the use of torture, but concluded that confessions were not obtained over cups of tea.

The secretary-general of Amnesty International has stated in an Israeli paper that there is no torture in Israeli jails and that the authorities are extremely strict about it. He went on to say that cases could arise of torture by persons not responsible to the prison authorities, members of the army for instance, or police

---

* Under the Jordanian regime, only a privileged minority were allowed to vote; but the Israelis have introduced *universal* suffrage and there are now thirty-five thousand Arab electors.

officers who might resort to brutality in their interrogations. There are blots on the copy-book, but they are more the exception than the rule and they are severely punished. As early in 1971, thirty Israeli officers and men were jailed for theft and extortion while searching Arab houses in Gaza. Opinions will vary with political colours, but smashed toes and broken bodies are blood-coloured. And I do not believe that torture is systematically employed in Israel. Public opinion wields a special power in Israel, where people are not numbed by words like 'prison' and 'torture', which stir other memories too recent and too terrible to be forgotten. The public demands firm action against abuses and those who commit them.

Unlike other Occupations, this one has a credit side. It is discreet, and does not continually better the minds or inflame old wounds. Nablus was in the grip of a general strike, yet there were only four armed soldiers sitting in a jeep on the edge of the town. M. Pierre Griaud, the socialist senator from Paris, once remarked, 'One meets fewer policemen in the Old City of Jerusalem than along the Boulevard Saint-Michel, and even though Israel is a country at war she doesn't put people in prison for airing the wrong views.' There is freedom of opinion, freedom of the press. When Nasser died, the Arabs paraded with portraits of the Bibakchi, and the Israeli authorities not only consented to the demonstrations, but were also on hand with Jordanian and Israeli police to protect the marchers.

Dayan believes in an economic solution first, in improving the economic condition of the occupied territories until they can integrate with Israel. He insists that the number of Arab workers must be doubled, and fosters the policy by which inhabitants of West-Bank Jordan can export their sheep and farm produce to the unoccupied side of the river. Agricultural advisers are available to Arab cultivators, and even the Bedouins are tending to settle down and make permanent homes for themselves. West-Bank Jordan has retained its own civil service, its own police force and its own broadcasting network, and until February 1971 the officials received salaries from both the Hashemite administration and the

Israeli authorities, which may explain their lack of ardour towards Al Fatah.

The traffic is not only in vegetables and sheep. Arabs tramp across the creaking boards of the Allenby bridge to invite their families on the West-Bank. Arab students in Jerusalem attend courses and sit examinations at the Hebrew University of the Hadassa – and the Israeli government was subsidising a large Palestinian university at Nablus, whose academic standards would be equal to those of the Hadassa.

Dayan, whose name is at the centre of any discussion of the Occupation, has an interesting and unusual background. A Sabra, (the name for a Jew born in Palestine), he grew up near Bedouin camps and played with Arab children as a small boy, even being comforted in their fathers' tents when the games got too rough. 'They are men of honour and I have a high regard for them,' he concluded. He speaks perfect Arabic and will intervene personally when serious incidents occur. He strode into the midst of rioting schoolchildren at Nablus, and went into the Casbahs at Ramallah and Gennin to negotiate with striking shopkeepers. He turned up to meet Sheikh el-Jabaari, the major of Hebron, in an open jeep with just a driver and two soldiers, unlike Hussein, who was always accompanied by half a dozen armoured cars. He had fired the imagination of the Palestinians I talked to with this courage and panache, recognized even in an enemy. Dayan's economic policy could cut the ground from under the feet of the terrorists (whose strength stems from the poverty of the refugee camps), and create an economic osmosis between West-Bank Jordan and Israel, a Common Market useful to both communities. He is liberal, intelligent and positive, and he can be very tough when security and public order are threatened. 'The *status quo* (is) crystallized', in Abba Eban's approbatory phrase and the 'faits accomplis'* multiply. Those Israelis who remember, hope passionately for security and settled frontiers and want no part in deeds that might be shady or acquisitive.

* e.g. a fishing village established on the northern coast of the Sinai peninsula and a score of kibbutzim set up in West-Bank Jordan and on the Golan heights.

The manager of the Dragon Hotel loudly disapproved of my plans. Nobody went to hot, deserted Egyptian, accursed Gaza except the army.

Gaza, this most troublesome land, is Israel's headache and the thorn in Dayan's side. It borders the Mediterranean, is nine miles across and thirty miles from end to end, and over half its area is sand. It is the only region where the Israeli forces wear helmets and truncheons. Occasional orange-trees punctuate the misery of more than five hundred and fifty thousand refugees parked in eight 'regroupment villages'. Until 1947, eighty thousand Gaza Arabs lived from fishing and meagre crops. In 1948, Egypt occupied the Strip and sluggishly administered the three hundred and twenty thousand Palestinian refugees who had fled from the conflict. Today the camps are run by the United Nations World Relief Administration, and food supplies are somewhat better. There is only one factory, which turns out packing-cases, and the Israeli authorities will not let the fishing-boats out since guerrillas, based in Egypt and the Lebanon, employed them to smuggle arms and ammunition. The camp-populations have stagnated in overcrowded misery for twenty years, housed in small cubes where a hen is a sign of wealth. Among the bitterness and discontent, the rival guerrilla organizations recruit collaborators to hurl crude, home-made grenades fashioned from beer-cans at army vehicles or Arabs on their way to work in Israel.

Although determined to clamp down on violence, Dayan is seeking a practical solution in the development of local industry with foundries, canning-factories, marmalade works. He believes that work and proper accommodation will transform the mental outlook in preparation for normal living. At the time of my visit, four thousand Palestinians, attracted by the high wages and social advantages, had moved out of the camps, turning their backs on twenty years of degradation to take jobs in Israel. They were often singled out by Al Fatah, but the guerrillas were powerless to prevent the growth of the industrial area north of Gaza.

Cars were rare, and, instead of troops and kibbutzniks, shadowy figures squatted in brown *galabiehs*. Peasant women, masked and shrouded in black, urged on their skinny donkeys, or balanced large earthware jars or aluminium drums of water.

The soldier with my Israeli number-plate waved me through. Young boys stared with hostility in a village of six shattered houses. The West had become an unjoyous East in five minutes.

Gaza is an Egyptian town of low, square, concrete houses, but there were bullet-holes everywhere. One house had been completely blasted, and many shops were barred and shuttered. Men in white *keffiehs,* grouped like a Delacroix painting, sat on the pavement, their backs to the street, puffing their hookahs. The occasional Israeli or Egyptian lorries of provisions were stopped and searched.

Rare cars carried white Egyptian number-plates. The shops were empty, the silence complete, the atmosphere could have been cut with a knife.

There were empty hotels, broken windows and garbage all along the esplanade. Youths hurled abuse after me. A girl screamed at her small brother who rashly came near me. The road narrowed in an increasing wretchedness of collapsed masonry, bullet-holes, and shrapnel scars. An old poster advertised United Arab Airlines. I wound up the windows for safety. In the market I stopped for some deep, glossy and splendid baskets, and the few shoppers were bemused to see a woman whom they took to be an Israeli wandering around buying baskets. Expressionless soldiers converged, their interest strictly professional. Only the urchins buzzed at me to buy counterfeit Chanel Number Five, counterfeit cigarettes, counterfeit Bic ballpoints, counterfeit sweets, and genuine oranges. Their eyes were bright, and even their parents became less hostile when they saw me as a meal-ticket.

Athletic young soldiers in black berets, with truncheons and fixed bayonets and leaden faces, patrolled the approaches to the market. Arab police were also patrolling, and everyone seemed poised for violence, with a stillness not of death but of waiting.

I was glad of my Israeli licence-plate and the privilege of getting out.

I drove east towards the Negev, past orchards and fields of wheat and barley farmed by Israeli Bedouins. Huts roofed with corrugated iron and permanent buildings have replaced traditional tents since the government's large-scale irrigation plans have channelled water from the Jordan to these desert tracts. The Bedouins have agricultural advisers, their cattle are vaccinated against foot-and-mouth disease and the old-fashioned plough with a single wooden share is disappearing before multi-furrow, deep-plough tractors.

In Israel, distances are short and a traveller can sample many different worlds on a simple journey. It was dark in Bersheeva, not a living town, but broad thoroughfares intersecting in the middle of nowhere, waiting, among the feather-duster palm-trees, for the built-up areas to come. The town-planning department lacked no imagination: they had the whole desert to grow in!

I lost my way on the featureless chessboard, and gave a lift to some hitch-hiking soldiers, thinking they would show me the way. I felt them freeze when I addressed them in French. They would not tell me where they were going, where they lived or where they were stationed*. Their strict orders certainly precluded talking to the shifty French. They stubbornly refused to direct me, and it was no thanks to them that I ever got to the hotel.

In the main thoroughfare dreadful concrete blocks rose high above the shops, a square with two tiled stone Turkish buildings, and a white mosque built from salvaged Byzantine stone.

The bovine blonde in 'reception' looked startlingly empty-headed, and my large room in the Desert Inn, Bersheeva, looked like a prison cell, with the concrete bars of its sun-break. I was rescued by my jovial friend Father Roger, shepherd of the local flock of six Catholics. He was an Assumptionist, about forty, balding but with a bushy-tailed grey beard stretching to his

* *'Les jeunes sots font les vieux cons.'* – Aragon.

powerful chest. He wore a short-sleeved shirt, or an old sweater
if the temperature fell below −20°. His brown eyes were always
smiling behind his round lenses. His deep, rich voice hailed me
from the entrance hall. Despite his small congregation, Jean-
Roger was father, ally and friend to everyone in the town. They
waved to him, shook his hand, smiled at him, talked to him, and
he answered them all. My grandmother would have called him in
Ladino, an *Alma del Dio,* a godly soul. He took me to a bistro in
a concrete cube built open to the road. Neon lights lit up the
plastic tables; the atmosphere was informal, very 'New-Frontier'.
The proprietor was descended from Sudanese slaves, and Jean-
Roger told me that, though he was a Moslem, he lived with a
Jewish woman and no one thought anything of it. Soldiers slung
their sub-machine-guns on the backs of their chairs or, like one
plump, red-headed girl, laid them carefully and neatly down. The
Bren-guns on their three jeeps parked outside the door pointed
towards the sky.

In the morning I swam in the pool. Rose-trees sprouted from the
surrounding sand, and noisy youngsters ran across the lawn,
contemptuous of the gardener who was combing it almost to
perfection.

Jean-Roger arrived, beard blowing in all directions. He was
taking me to Arad by car and then to Masada.

The road, lined with mimosa, ran straight across the almost
barren plain. We passed large, black, rectangular tents with
glimpses of Bedouin life beyond their raised awnings.
Occasionally there were shacks instead of tents, and I wondered
aloud if this were progress. But Jean-Roger had an unshakeable
love for the Negev and might have argued that Bersheeva was
more beautiful than Paris. Enthusiastically he talked about
excavations, revealing that in the Paleolithic era the land was
farmed by stable communities. Moreover, the desert plain, making up one fifth of the Negev and one tenth of Israel, was
partially covered with a loamy deposit which needs only irrigation
to yield an abundance of cereals and fruit-trees.

There was a Peugeot 404 parked outside a tent, a television aerial jutting from a corrugated iron roof. And as in Mexico, there were cactus agaves but they were used to make rope rather than the vile fermented *pulque* of the Mexican Indians.

The desert became grey plateaux, flecked with colour, a few goats, a benign camel browsing on the gorse. The sky was harsh blue and the air light and fresh.

We reached Arad with scorching eyes. Today twelve thousand people live in a town wrested from the desert in ten years by building concrete blocks for them to live in. I sank down on the steps of the main square, overlooking the maze of incomplete buildings rising, without any green, from the sand and volcanic craters. With our little linen hats, we covered our heads in the scorching spring heat. Jean-Roger marvelled at everything, with no idea of what time the coach left or where from. I left him dreaming while I looked at the little museum with odds and ends from Masada geological specimens, reconstructed pottery and Neolithic lumps, and a touching display of local painting and sculpture drawing beauty from an arid environment.

Jean-Roger was still sitting, as unconcerned as ever about our journey. I found our coach overcrowded and about to leave. I hurried Jean-Roger and we clambered aboard, crushing an American family in our efforts to find an inch or two of seat.

Masada dominates the Dead Sea, a great tooth-like rock rising sheer from the valley. It is a shrine of Israel, where each intake of army officers swears the oath of allegiance; it is where the thousand Zealots, after desperately resisting the Romans, were cornered by the Legions of Flavius Silva and, rather than be captured alive, chose to be killed by ten of their number, who afterwards committed suicide. It is a symbol of a never-ending spiritual struggle and the embodiment of resistance.

We climbed to the fortress, following the stone ramp which the Romans built to capture the citadel. Mercifully, steps have been cut and there are guard-rails. Half way up we encountered Father Gélin, whose eloquence on this occasion was directed at four young Germans with hobnailed shoes and grey *lederhosen*.

He included us in his lecture, until the long queues of pilgrims and tourists above and below us made him realize that he had chosen an odd place to create a bottleneck.

For me there was Herod's ghost dwelling among the pillars and mosaics and faded frescoes, rather than echoes of the luckless Zealots. The mountains around us glowed against an apocalyptic sky, and a flock of storks flew level with us. At first they seemed ten, then a hundred, then a thousand. They hovered round the ruins, flapping black and white wings like veils. The Moslems called the Stork Gate in Jerusalem *Laklak*. The birds cried raucously to one another. Jean-Roger was in ecstasy with his camera. The birds were going north to Russia; the sky was black with them, and still they came, wave after wave, mustering their order.

Ygael Yadin rescued the fortress from the sand and the deposits of centuries by launching an appeal in 1963, rallying students and volunteers from every country, to sleep in makeshift quarters, eat Kosher food and toil in the blazing sun.

We drove along the Dead Sea among outcrops of salt to Sodom, where the level of the water has fallen a hundred and fifty feet since the Tertiary Period. Past a big potassium work, we paid our respects to Lot's wife, turned to salt when the Lord rained brimstone and fire on the Cities of the Plain. Jean-Roger read the passage from Genesis and its spicy aftermath. Lot's two daughters, unlike their mother, didn't look back. With no other man to turn to, they plied their father with drink and 'lay with him'. From this villainous coupling came Moab, the first of the Moabites, who settled in the mountains across the lake, and Ben-ammi, 'father of the Ammanites', who peopled the region of Amman. It is said that the girls' misdoings sowed the perennial hatred of the Israelis and the Jordanians.

The landscape darkened with a yellow haze and a scorching wind began to whip about us. It was the 'ninth Plague of Egypt', a sandstorm, and the air grew darker, yellow and grey; the sand rustled and soon we needed headlamps. I glimpsed a Bedouin crouching under a tree whose branches clapped wildly in the wind.

In 1880, Trappists first dug into the desert soil of Latrun, today the grounds of their monastery are thick with fragrant oaks, pines, olives and oranges. Above the olive-trees, the hill is crowned by the ruins of a Frankish Templar fortress dismantled by Saladin in 1187. I tugged at the bellpull and loud peals echoed from somewhere overhead. Father Emile arrived, lean, ascetic, with the celestial smile of a Flemish primitive.

The abbey was unrelieved white with a roof of circular tiles, like a country house in Provence. The monks cultivate five hundred acres of vineyards and rent some land to a neighbouring kibbutz. They also provide work for Arab labourers who came to them when the Jews demolished two Arab villages in the plain, where the kibbutz is today. The Trappists' income is chiefly from the sale of wine. There used to be regular markets in Palestine and Jordan, and there were few vineyards then, but now they have sprung up all over the place and the Jordanian market is closed. The monks are on excellent terms with the Israelis, and get large numbers of Israeli tourists every Saturday. But they remember being knocked about a bit, in 1948, when the monastery got two direct hits, and in 1967 when they got seven more. The Israelis were trying to dislodge Jordanians from the fortress, though in fact they had already fled. The Israeli commander called at the monastery to present his apologies. He told the monks that he had been a split second too late in noticing his gunners' sights on the monastery.

Archaeological fragments were set on the terrace in the shade of magnificent trees and flowers and ivy-mantled walls. The Father Superior, Dom Elie Businier, showed us the chapel, parlour and library, all peaceful, noble, and smelling sweet with polish. He was once a top-flight tennis-player and had been at Latrun for the past thirty-six years. The mother-house had been tempted to close the monastery after the Six-Day War, as it was no longer used to spread the Gospel and their mission would thrive better in a Moslem setting, but the Israelis, who tolerate existing religious establishments, will not allow any new ones, and the monks are staying put.

The car was giving trouble, but where in the suburbs of Tel Aviv, among a hodge-podge of petrol pumps, high-rise flats and untidy stretches of waste ground, could one find an Alfa mechanic? The old Turkish houses have fallen into disrepair and are adorned with battered oil-drums more often than with geranium pots. Eventually, in front of a building half-garage, half-workshop, I found a man tackling the engine of a lorry. His arms were smothered with oil, but he looked rather smart in a black sweater and grey flannels as he emerged from under the bonnet and greeted me coolly. His wife, who made us coffee, was from Vienna and he from Berlin. She was a tall, distinguished-looking woman with short grey hair and alert nut-brown eyes. They were very young when they arrived in Palestine in the 1930s. Though he had studied engineering he could speak no Hebrew and, like many of his generation, he had to take a job with a lower standard of living. In Israel, social status is not derived, as it is elsewhere, from the manner in which one earns one's bread.

His wife understood the problems of the Arab workers, though they were materially so much better off, and they mainly feared that further Arab-Israeli clashes would prevent them from working in Tel Aviv. The position of Israeli Arabs is materially enviable but ambiguous. There were four hundred thousand Arabs in Israel's pre-1967 frontiers; they had the same privileges as Jews, with schools, hospitals, social security and high wages, and were much better off than other Arabs. This equality was not shared by the Arabs of Jerusalem, but even their position was better than that of the inhabitants of the occupied terrritories. Israeli Arabs had advantages over the Jews, as they paid no income-tax and were exempt, for obvious reasons, from military service.

Having lived so closely with the Jews for almost thirty years so that they can speak Hebrew learned in the same schools, these people have acquired a western outlook and made bonds of friendship and affection inevitable when peoples' lives are thrown together. But their destiny as Arabs was still inextricably bound up with that of their 'brothers', as they were reminded night and day by the propaganda broadcasts from Amman and Cairo, which called on them to join the Holy War in acts of terrorism.

The engineer announced his diagnosis. 'Every man to his own trade,' he said. 'You worry about your book and I'll deal with your car.'

In the hullabaloo of the Hilton, amid the green plants and fat American ladies, the loudspeaker system was calling Mr Winston Churchill to the telephone.

The sky had clouded and it was soon pelting down, so I stayed in the hairdresser's. The energetic, fat, little Moroccan stylist talked about his recent spell of military duty. Unlikely as it seemed, he had been attached to a patrol unit, then transferred to the heavy artillery, and ended up as a frogman. With an army of all-rounders, troops could be rushed anywhere, as the soldiers' skills were interchangeable. After full-time military service they were on reserve and recalled for a month or so each year. Officers had to do fifty-two days a year, other ranks forty-three. He thought it terrific, meeting old friends and being really fit by the end of it.

'Jaffa has been admirably restored,' they told me. And so it has, if you like four-square buildings, all in the pervasive pink of sugared almonds, and a proliferation of boutiques with arty fabrics, clever ironwork, and bad paintings.

Behind the waterfront is a slum, where the proud Phoenician city which fell to Rameses II is reduced to unpaved streets turned to mud from burst water-mains. The once-beautiful Turkish houses are black and open to the winds, patched with cardboard and corrugated iron. Beyond are the ill-lit hotels of the new immigrants from the Yemen and the poorest *mellahs* of North Africa.

Before the Six-Day War these usually poor and illiterate 'oriental' immigrants were ostracized, and people were angered that the young Moroccans attending the overcrowded universities of Tel Aviv and Jerusalem would return home after their studies, using degrees, which they could never have obtained in their own country, as passports to social advancement paid for by the Israeli government. Conscription and compulsory education are great levellers. These divisions died away afterwards, but flared up again in 1971 when the Israeli government started to woo engineers, doctors, scientists. Because of the Soviet restrictions on Jewish emigration these intellectuals came mainly from the West, especially America*, and were accustomed to a fairly high standard of living. As an inducement, they were guaranteed suitable jobs, good accommodation and adequate salaries.

The more militant young Yemenites and North Africans have banded together in activist groups against this preferential treatment; known as 'Black Panthers', they have strong links with the left-wing Matzpen party and with a number of declared Communists, and are bent on causing the government as much trouble as possible.

The vast, ultra-modern hall, decorated with wood and concrete, was packed to capacity. It was a Leonard Bernstein concert. Sitting in front of me was Golda Meir, younger, gentler, smaller and less formidable than her photographs, in tailored yellow and smiling broadly. The lady was with her ministers and friends, Herzogs, Dinsteins, Tsurs, Avigdars – all smiling faces milling in my mind.

Bernstein makes a pretence of mockery at our enthusiasm. Who cares! He is an unchained virtuoso, clown and poet, talented and witty.

Later the Maestro was received at the Hotel Dan. Here, surrounded by many friends, he was given a grand, warm welcome by Kessel, handsome and leonine, and Golda Meir, nodding kindly, before a discreet departure. The assembly of top-level

* Ben Gurion used to hope that the mood of unrest among young people in the United States would prompt many Jews in their teens and twenties to make new homes in Israel. Their presence, he felt, would offset the orientalizing influence of the Iraqis, Yemenites and Moroccans. 'We have room for five million Americans,' he claimed.

politicians, intellectuals, generals and bankers was like a bourgeois marriage feast in France: the men wore dark suits, and the women in their sober best, with one or two dream-like sirens from the world of cinema and fashion swathed in exotic folds. One was aware that, as at Cinderella's ball, all this gaiety and glamour would cease early, for everyone would work tomorrow and even the wives of these important men had important things to do. Prices are high but salaries are not, even at the top, and it is hard to live on one income. Life is tough on these well-groomed ladies when staff is as rare as it is expensive and children can't bring themselves up. Boredom is unknown, but anxiety is often there. An eldest son is on the Canal, a youngest in the Golan. They must often wake up, those smiling ladies, and worry through the dark hours of the night.

Shalhevet Freiar, a charming young physicist, took me to the Weizmann Institute.

The library had 'No Smoking' signs and ashtrays everywhere, and the laboratory, for research in the acceleration of molecules was full of tubes and panels and dials.

Shalhevet, after tortuous expositions in French, reverted to English to explain that only a third of their finance came from the Government, the rest depended on research contracts. The Institute had discreet but substantial contracts with French companies. The fact that it was nearly self-supporting made it free of government dictation though the ill-formed opinions of its generous donors often caused embarrassment to the scientists.

Shalhevet admitted that pure scientific research carried to excess, stifles imagination. Against this danger, the Institute encourages industries of a scientific nature to set up nearby and to use its research facilities. Scientists thus had the experience of seeing their work put into effect, and industrialists could draw on the intellectual bank to solve their technical problems.

My friend Ehud Avriel, the genial gun-runner of 1948 from the kibbutz at Nehot Mordecai, asked me to meet him at the Dan Hotel at seven next morning. I thought it a little early, but he insisted. I asked to be allowed at least a coffee. But, no, the surprise was breakfast with Dayan.

We took a taxi to a tree-lined street and stopped beside a Land-Rover whose occupants were obviously bodyguards. Dayan appeared, bounding across the road, greeting Ehud with affection, smiling broadly and shaking me warmly by the hand. He wore a tan shirt and khaki trousers, and looked shorter and tubbier than I imagined him, as he ushered us into the drawing-room lined with books and finds which reflected his passionate interest in archaelogy and the regular visits of the Arab dealers in Jerusalem. A large bay-window opened to a patio, where a stele was framed by two Roman columns. Mrs Dayan, about fifty, stout, with a pale, full, handsome face framed by dark hair, announced breakfast.

I was on the General's right with an intimate view of the famous eye-patch. This, held by a black cord around his head, bothered him to the point of agitation. He fiddled with it, moving it a fraction of an inch this way and that. He was cheerful, friendly, sun-tanned: a simple man without affectation.

'I don't often meet French people nowadays; I appreciate my good fortune all the more. France has done us some harm in the past few years, but no amount of harm can equal the good she once did us. That is something we shall never forget.'

It was a heartfelt tribute. Ehud joked about the Mirages, and Dayan said the substitute American Phantoms were very sound and relatively easy to handle. 'But you know,' he concluded with a laugh, 'we prefer the subtlety, virtuosity and complexity of the French.'

We talked about King Abdullah, Sherif Hussein's son, disliked by Lawrence and sold short by the British with the artificial kingdom of Transjordan. Dayan had known him well during the fighting in 1948 and the negotiations before the proclamation of the State of Israel. He spoke of him with respect and admiration and a special brand of fellow-feeling for an esteemed adversary.

'A great king, a very intelligent man, courageous and chivalrous.' And Mrs Dayan went into ecstasies about him. 'A wonderful person, the very essence of charm; I've never met anyone with such exquisite manners. I'm almost sorry he's not here!'

Of necessity our farewells were brief. The General's car was waiting and Mrs Dayan had to get to her office at the National Fashion House.

Ehud insisted that if people knew how sensitive Dayan was he would lose his absurd reputation for harshness. He told me of Dayan arriving late and exhausted for dinner, having spent the day with the troops in the Canal Zone, deafened by the roar of the Egyptian artillery. Turning to Ehud with tears in his eyes, he had said, 'You cannot imagine what hell it is for those boys. I don't mind telling you, it keeps me awake at night.'

Another dawn departure. I was being taken flying by Jerry, a Second-War pilot who now did a bit of everything: ferrying, stunt-flying, spraying insecticides. We headed towards Sinai, which I motored across in the days when I organized Egyptian tours for Connaissance des Arts; my flock and I would camp at Abu Zenima, on the shores of the Red Sea.

In fifteen minutes we were over Jerusalem: the Kedron, the Valley of Jehoshaphat, the Mount of Olives. These legendary places which so many people have fought for looked insignificant from the air. The banking of the aircraft, as we swept down to take our photographs, put a queasy end to such thoughts. Less than a sigh away was Masada where we flew past like the storks of my recent visit. It was getting hot, but we continued south over the Negev, where a tiny patch of green among the ochre marked a kibbutz, and so on to Sinai: first the sands, then mauve cliffs, then mountains, and finally the pinnacle of the Jebel Katherina. We banked port, starboard, port again, and dived for a 'good view' of the monastery. I shut my eyes.

'What say we fly above the mountains?' I suggested weakly, staring at the jagged walls of rock only yards away.

'I don't think that's possible,' Jerry returned calmly. 'Some are over nine thousand feet, which is about twice my maximum.'

I wondered what my own maximum was; I felt I had nearly reached it.

The fantastic landscape calmed me with its ochre walls, violet gorges, and needles of blue like perpendicular rays pointing towards the monastery.

We turned away, fast and low across the desert, and landed at Eilat in the humid noon heat. The harbour peers across the narrow gulf-head at its Jordanian neighbour, Aqaba, not eyeball to eyeball, but with a continuous sidelong glance.

Ignoring the oil patches on the sand, I strode like a sleep-walker into the cool water. I soaked it into every pore until my movements grew lighter and quicker. I plunged deep, my mouth full of the murky Red Sea.

There had been much debate, so much time, so many people, so much landscape, so many cities; and I still feel a thirst for Palestine.

When I hear bold assertions and passionate opinions, I remember a face from the other camp. I stay quiet, a little sad, a little envious, like an atheist confronting faith, hoping only that things will work out, knowing that they won't but praying in despair that no one will die.

# Index

185